KATIE BROWN'S
WEEKENDS

KATIE BROWN'S
WEEKENDS

MAKING THE MOST OF YOUR TWO TREASURED DAYS

PHOTOGRAPHY BY PAUL WHICHELOE

Bulfinch Press
NEW YORK · BOSTON

Bulfinch Press

Time Warner Book Group
1271 Avenue of the Americas
New York, NY 10020
Visit our Web site at www.bulfinchpress.com

First Edition: October 2005

Library of Congress Cataloging-in-Publication Data

Brown, Katie.
    Katie Brown's weekends : making the most of your
two treasured days / Katie Brown ; photography by
Paul Whicheloe.—1st ed.
        p. cm.
    ISBN 0-8212-6209-2
1. Cookery. I. Title.
    TX714.B78 2005
    641.5—dc22

2005011366

Design: Empire Design Studio

Printed in the United States of America

CONTENTS

INTRODUCTION

Every Friday we would pack up the car and travel to my grandparents' house. We would arrive just in time for my father to attend his high school's Friday night football game. Saturday was spent visiting with my thirty-two first cousins and fourteen aunts and uncles, and Sunday morning was a big waffle breakfast and then off to church. *Monday always came too soon.* Then I got busy: for my sisters and I ski races would occupy our weekends. Friday night was for waxing the equipment, and Saturday and Sunday were spent competing. *Monday always came too soon.* Then college: parties, studying, talking. *Monday always came too soon.*

My first job out of college as an executive trainee at Saks Fifth Avenue often required me to work Friday nights. I sometimes found myself in the office on Sundays as well. *Monday always came too soon.* When I ran a catering company, I would develop the menu, shop, and cook the food all week. The weekends were spent serving the food and working at the event. *Monday always came too soon.* Now as a TV show producer and host, author, mother, and wife, Monday seems no different from any other day — weekend or no weekend. Mondays never seem to come, and my two days that had traditionally been set aside to enjoy my family and accomplish things that strike my fancy have now been replaced with, well, quite simply, work. I get melancholy just thinking about the long-gone years of active Saturdays and lazy Sundays. Why and how had I let them slip away, only to replace them with the repetition of another workday? Just another day to accomplish a few more things on my to-do lists.

As I began reflecting and investigating the answer to this question, I found I am not alone. In the United States much has been written recently about our nation's work habits and the shrinking weekends of our citizens. We have surpassed Japan in the number of hours that make up our workweek. Fewer and fewer of us are taking advantage of our time off.

I used to say as a self-effacing comment that I am a workaholic, but secretly I was quite proud of that fact. You see, I love what I do. But the more I pushed myself, the more I found my work suffered. It became stale and redundant when I wasn't taking the time to do the things I love. I became moody and less accomplished as I continued on day twelve of being a worker bee. No more; I had to find a way to take back my two treasured days, but I really didn't know how to break the habit of working all the time.

How do I turn off the work brain and stop the lists of chores from rattling around in my head? How can I discontinue the trend of the last ten years and decrease my time spent working on the weekends? I've learned that come Friday night, I need a plan — a blueprint, if you will — of what my weekend will look like. So I pick a fun or timely theme and run with it. Some themes are broader than others, such as *rejuvenate,* a weekend spent pampering myself and my family; or perhaps something more specific like *apple picking,* a weekend spent collecting fall's harvest, then turning its fruits into pies, butter, or stamps for tablecloths. Yes, this works by giving me a pleasurable goal. This workaholic has become quite blissful with her weekend retreats. The more complete my weekends have become, the more productive my workweeks are. I have found ways to spend more time with those I love and rejuvenate my home on my Saturdays and Sundays. And alas, again, *Mondays are coming much too soon.*

Throughout this book I hope you will find ideas and inspirations to reclaim or simply reinvent your weekends. Discover the satisfaction of lending a *Helping Hand.* Simplify your life by channeling your inner *Neat Freak.* Find peace in your *Secret Garden.* Revitalize yourself in the *Great Outdoors.* Expand yourself by sampling treats from *Around the World.* And shine from the glow of a glamorous *Holiday.* These are just the beginning of ways you can form new habits in order to join what I hope is a new trend to take back our two treasured days.

Words like *charity, giving,* and *helping* seem to make everyone sit up, stand up, raise their hand, and say, "Yes, where do I sign up? How can I begin?" You want to get started, and you want to get started right then and there. But alas, you must sign up . . . you must go through training . . . they are not taking volunteers at this time. What is one to do who is eager to give back to the world around them? I say it is possible to quickly indulge your goodwill if you keep in mind the phrase my mother would so often recite to me: "Blossom where you are planted." This was her response when I complained of boredom as a youth in my little hometown of Petoskey, Michigan.

"There is nowhere worth blossoming around these lonely streets," I would say as I rolled my eyes in frustration. Then I would smell something delectable coming from our kitchen. It appeared my mother had baked a few more batches of her homemade cinnamon bread. She asked me to get on my bike and deliver the sweet loaves to our neighbor, Mrs. Alm. I sped off on my banana-seat bike with my basket full, leaving a trail of the sweet smell of cinnamon. Mrs. Alm was an older woman whose husband had suffered a stroke. Knock, knock . . . knock knock . . . no answer. Then I heard a voice from behind the house. "I am around back," the voice said. I fetched the still-warm bread from my basket and hurried around to the backyard. Wow. I had never seen anything like this. It looked like a scene described in the novel *The Secret Garden:* tall, Amazonlike flowers, "Jack in the Beanstalk"–type vines, with Mrs. Alm kneeling in the moss patch, digging in the dirt, wearing a hat twice the size of her head. "My mom asked me to give you this bread."

"Well, won't that just cheer the old man up. Thank your mother for me," she said with a gracious smile. Then she asked me if wanted to look around in her "enchanted forest."

Oh, the fun I had twisting in and around Mrs. Alm's green friends! So, you see, my mother enlisting me as her good-deed partner proved to resurrect my very dull afternoon. Look around your own neighborhood next time the do-gooder spirit moves you. Maybe enlist the help of a friend or encourage your children to get involved. Make a day or, better yet, a weekend of it. You will be surprised at how much you will blossom when you tend to people in need — especially those who live just alongside where you are planted.

the art of supporting those in need

HELPING HANDS

BLOCK PARTY

I remember when the garden club would fill the neighborhood flower boxes and plant the roadsides in Petoskey. The buzz of the town grew happier, and the sidewalks were more crowded when the colorful blooms were artistically placed throughout our streets. So how about taking a cue from the ladies' auxiliary and organize a fulfilling twist on a neighborhood party? From planting gardens to painting walls, enjoy a weekend of sprucing up the block with your friends and family. Include everyone — no matter how big or how small, there is always room for all.

How Does Your
Garden Grow?

Add some life and beauty to a part of town that needs some TLC. Consider planting some tulips in a tub or begonias in a bureau.

TOOLS
spade
garden gloves
garden rake

MATERIALS
discarded furniture or fixtures
wood chips
soil
plants

1.   Make sure the piece you're using as a planter has a drainage hole. For example, a tub has a drain, file cabinets do not, so you will need to create a hole in the bottom of each drawer that will house your plants.

2.   Fill the planter approximately halfway with bark chips.

3.   Fill your object another third of the way with soil.

4.   Tip the pots upside down and gently pull the plants out of their pots and use your fingers or a rake to break up the root ball a bit. (This will help their transition from pot to garden.)

5.   Place your plants in the planter and fill it all the way up with soil.

6.   Water your new garden thoroughly.

KEEP IT SIMPLE Consult your local garden center for tips on what will thrive under your growing conditions.

YOU CAN'T GO WRONG Plant your garden seasonally. For example, we planted a summer bathtub with ferns and primrose, a winter tire with inkberry and flowering heather, and an autumn file cabinet with crotons, begonias, ivy, and rosemary.

You'll need a lot of hands (and mops) for this project, but don't worry, we're not cleaning, just painting! Wrap your mops in terry cloth and let the towels do the talkin' to a wall that really needs it!

Picnic, Paint, & Prettify!

TOOLS

string mops

paint buckets or trays

MATERIALS

terry-cloth towels

heavy-duty rubber bands

colorful paints

scrap paper or newspaper for blotting

Combine the following two techniques to create a colorful abstract mural.

TECHNIQUE #1

1. Wrap the mop end of the mop with a towel. Secure the towel with a rubber band.

2. Dip the towel in paint and blot it on the wall in an abstract arrangement.

TECHNIQUE #2

1. Trim the strings of the mop down to approximately 4 inches in length.

2. Dip the mop into the paint, blot any excess paint on scrap paper or newspaper, dot the mop randomly over the wall.

Italian Tuna Salad
Sandwich

SERVES 8

INGREDIENTS

2 12-ounce cans solid white albacore
    tuna in water, drained

1 rib celery, chopped

1/2 small red onion, finely chopped

1/4 cup chopped black olives

2 tablespoons chopped fresh basil

1/2 cup bottled Italian dressing

1 loaf round bread

1. Toss together the tuna, celery, onion, olives, and basil in a large bowl with the Italian dressing until mixed.

2. Slice the round loaf in half horizontally and hollow out the bottom half.

3. Spread tuna mixture evenly into the hollowed-out area, replace the top half of the loaf, and press down firmly.

4. For individual sandwiches, slice the loaf in half crosswise, then into wedges.

Potato Salad
with Chives

SERVES 8

INGREDIENTS

24 new potatoes

4 teaspoons apple cider vinegar

2 tablespoons minced chives

10 tablespoons sour cream

salt and pepper

2 cups apples, cut into bite-size pieces

1/2 cup raisins

1. Place potatoes in a large pot and cover with cold water. Bring to a boil and cook until potatoes are done — 10–15 minutes, depending on size of potato. Quarter potatoes, or halve if smaller potatoes, after they are cooked.

2. In a large bowl, whisk together vinegar, chives, and sour cream. Season with salt and pepper to taste.

3. Add the potatoes, apples, and raisins to the dressing while still warm, and toss thoroughly to coat.

Plymouth Turkey
Sandwich

SERVES 8

A crowd is a crowd is a crowd, but a happy crowd is a full crowd. So keep your team moving by filling their bellies with yummy and inventive food that travels well.

INGREDIENTS

8 ounces cream cheese, at room temperature

1 cup cranberry preserves

1 tablespoon finely chopped fresh sage

salt and pepper

16 slices whole wheat bread

1 pound smoked turkey or roasted turkey breast, thinly sliced

16 Boston lettuce leaves

1.   Using a mixer, mix together cream cheese, ½ cup of cranberry preserves, and sage in a medium bowl until fluffy. Season with salt and pepper to taste.

2.   Spread each slice of bread with about 1 tablespoon of the cream cheese mixture. Divide the turkey and lettuce among 8 slices of the bread. Top with additional cranberry preserves and a second slice of bread.

Ruby Slaw

SERVES 8

INGREDIENTS

6 cups red cabbage, shredded

1 medium red onion, thinly sliced

1/2 cup dried cherries

1/4 cup raspberry vinegar

3/4 cup olive oil

1 tablespoon red raspberry preserves

salt and pepper

1. In a large bowl, toss together cabbage, onion, and dried cherries. Set aside.

2. Whisk vinegar and oil together until blended. Season with salt and pepper to taste.

3. Add the raspberry preserves to the vinaigrette and mix well. Pour over the slaw and toss to coat. Cover and chill.

YES, YOU CAN For this recipe, you can substitute red wine vinegar for the raspberry vinegar.

KEEP IT SIMPLE You can buy packages of preshredded cabbage.

Caramel Pecan
Brownies

SERVES 8

INGREDIENTS

1 box brownie mix

24 whole pecans

9 caramels

2 tablespoons milk

1. Prepare brownie mix according to package. Spread into a baking pan. Top with pecans and bake as directed.

2. Combine caramels with milk and melt on the stove over low heat.

3. When brownies are done baking, remove them from the oven and drizzle caramel over them.

Iced Tea

SERVES 8

Earl Grey with Lemon Mint Syrup

INGREDIENTS

For Syrup

1 cup water

1 cup sugar

1 cup mint

1 lemon, zested and torn into pieces

lemon slices for garnish

For Tea

8 cups water

7 Earl Grey tea bags

FOR LEMON-MINT SYRUP

1. In a saucepan, combine water, sugar, mint, and lemon zest and pieces.

2. Bring to a boil and stir to dissolve sugar. Reduce heat and simmer for 2 minutes.

3. Remove from heat, cool, and strain, pressing hard on the mint and lemon.

FOR ICED TEA

1. Bring 4 cups of water to a boil, pour over the tea bags, and steep for 6 minutes.

2. Add 4 cups of cold water. Chill.

3. Add syrup to taste.

Apricot Mint

INGREDIENTS

10 tea bags

8 cups water

12 ounces apricot nectar

$1/2$ cup mint leaves

$1/4$ cup sugar

mint sprigs for garnish

apricots for garnish

1. Boil 4 cups water, pour over the tea bags, and let steep for 6 minutes.

2. Add 4 cups of cold water, apricot nectar, mint leaves, and sugar. Stir to dissolve sugar.

3. Chill for a few hours. Strain before serving.

LEMONADE
50¢
$DONATED

LEMONADE STAND

What kid does not love a lemonade stand? This old kid is no exception. When I drive through the streets of my neighborhood, my heart starts fluttering at the mere sight of a sign in the distance. I am reminded of my entrepreneurial days on Mitchell Street, selling pitcher after pitcher. I would meet my neighbors as they left the shelter of their homes to try my brew. Believe it or not, the best part of my early self-employed days was when my mother would have us send a portion of our earnings to sponsor a needy child. Months later I would relive my joyous day at the lemonade stand when a letter, a drawing, or a report card would come in from my sponsored child. It filled me with pride to respond to my pen pal. There would be more where that came from next year, thanks to the support and generosity of my next-door patrons. So you don't have to go far to dedicate your weekend to helping others. This particular project can be a fun family affair that will instill in your children the thrill of making and sharing a buck. Spend Saturday cooking and constructing and leave Sunday to collecting. Then count your dollars and choose your children's cause.

Apron o' Pouches

When the kids are running the show at the lemonade stand, this handy waist pouch is a must-have to help them organize their tools, trash, and earnings.

TOOLS

hot-glue gun

knife

paint brush

MATERIALS

canvas waist pouch

decorative ribbon

1 large lemon

paper towels

yellow fabric paint

black permanent marker

1. Cut off the canvas strings or waist ties from sides of the pouch.

2. Hot-glue ribbon along the top edge of pouch, leaving an extra foot or more on either side to act as a belt.

3. Cut the lemon in half lengthwise and pat one half dry with a paper towel.

4. Lightly paint the cut side of the lemon and stamp it on the waist pouch to decorate.

5. Using a black permanent marker, outline the lemon shape and the interior outline of the fruit on the pouch.

Make a stand and make a difference!

Sweets, tarts, & hearts

TOOLS
tape measure

scissors

pinking shears

MATERIALS
4 yards of fabric (or old sheets or curtains)

2 2 x 2 x 84-inch wooden poles

2 2 x 2 x 72-inch wooden poles

4 curtain rod finials

4 large buckets

sand

lemons (optional)

1. Attach the front corners of the fabric to the two 6-foot-tall poles by screwing the finials through the fabric into the wood.

2. Measuring back approximately 5 feet, attach the fabric to the two 7-foot-tall poles using the finials in the same way. (Let the remainder of the fabric hang down in between the two back poles.)

3. Fill your four buckets with sand and ground your poles into the buckets to keep your tent sturdy.

DID YOU KNOW? Finials are most commonly used on the ends of curtain rods.

YOU CAN'T GO WRONG Using pinking sheers, cut a slit up the middle of the hanging fabric. This becomes the "curtain" for the stand, behind which you can store your supplies.

MAKE IT CHIC Cover the surface of the sand with piles of lemons.

Drinks for Dimes!

Advertising is a *must* when your kids are trying to sell their refreshments, so help them make as much moolah as you can by constructing this simple but compelling sign!

TOOLS
hammer

MATERIALS
3 kraft-wood panels (6 x 24")

wooden garden stake

small brads

colored painter's tape

1. Lay the stake on the ground and place the three kraft-wood panels parallel to one another on the stake, leaving one inch between panels.

2. Nail 2 brads into each panel, about ¼ inch from the top and ¼ inch from the bottom. This will keep the panel from rotating.

3. Use the painter's tape to write the text on your sign.

Lemonades

Remember that house on the block that had the best Halloween candy? I would alter my route to be sure to hit that house, no matter how far away it was. The same is true for the best lemonade stand in the neighborhood. Gussy up your juice and flavor your sicles so that there are more dimes collected for the cause.

Pink Lemonade

SERVES 8

INGREDIENTS

1 cup lemon juice, freshly squeezed or bottled

1 cup strawberries, sliced

$1/2$ cup sugar

5 cups water

lemon slices (optional)

1. In a blender, puree lemon juice and strawberries. Strain through fine mesh strainer, pressing berries with spatula.

2. Combine juice, sugar, and water and stir until sugar is dissolved. Pour into a jar and cover. Refrigerate. Add lemon slices, if desired, before serving.

Blueberry Lemonade

SERVES 8

INGREDIENTS

$3 1/2$ cups water

$1/2$ cup blueberry jam

$1/2$ cup sugar

$1 1/4$ cups lemon juice, freshly squeezed

lemon slices (optional)

1 package blueberries, fresh or frozen (optional)

1. In a pot, heat water, jam, and sugar until jam and sugar have dissolved. Remove from heat and let cool for 20 minutes.

2. Add lemon juice to sugar-and-jam mixture. Pour into a jar and cover. Refrigerate. Add blueberries and/or lemon slices, if desired, before serving.

MATERIALS

6 paper cups

aluminum foil

6 Popsicle sticks

INGREDIENTS

2 cups milk

$1/2$ cup heavy cream

1 package white chocolate or vanilla (4-serving size) instant pudding mix

3–5 drops red or blue food coloring (optional)

1 cup blueberries, strawberries, or raspberries, fresh or frozen

1. In a blender, combine milk, heavy cream, and pudding mix. Blend until smooth.

2. For blue or pink pops, add food coloring now. Blend until combined.

3. Let stand for 5 minutes, then stir in berries.

4. Pour into paper cups.

5. Cover each cup with foil and cut a slit in foil to insert a Popsicle stick.

6. Freeze for 4 hours or overnight.

Frozen Berry Pudding Pops

MAKES 6 POPSICLES

GOOD NEIGHBOR

When I was eleven years old, my mom broke her leg in twelve places. It seemed like she was bedridden for almost a year, and the one thing that cheered us up was the generosity of our kind neighbors. Without our knowing, they had gotten together to figure out how the Brown family was going to eat warm meals with our household chef incapacitated. So each night a different neighbor would appear on our doorstep with a hot dinner packaged in a beautiful traveling basket. Their actions truly helped inspire this chapter. I also hope that when you get the urge to reach out, you remember to look no further than over your own fence or to your very own friends and family.

Whether you are welcoming a new neighbor or nursing a friend back to health, you can begin by picking up the phone and organizing your neighborhood posse. All you need is a sign-up clipboard to organize your schedule and menus, a spruced-up basket, and an arsenal of simple recipes that will reheat easily. Or, for the new neighbor on the block, compile a book of favorite local restaurants to share.

You can also be neighborly by putting something festive or welcoming on your front door. Then people like my mother will slow down as they drive by, smile, and say, "Now, isn't she working hard at being a good neighbor."

Won't You Be
My Neighbor?

I was always jealous of the new girl in school. She had all the attention from the boys, and me, I was just the same old same old Katie. Never a new town, never a new school, never a new neighborhood. Now, as a mature grown-up, I understand that the new girl in school must have felt awkward, uncomfortable, and homesick. So I have transformed my jealousy into generosity by inventing my own version of the welcome wagon: a welcome-to-the-neighborhood guidebook. I spend Saturday gathering all my secrets and Sunday placing the treasures in a package that will acquaint any newcomer with their new surroundings.

TOOLS

straightedge

craft glue

scissors

hole punch

camera

MATERIALS

2 precut 12 x 12-inch
kraft-wood panels

heavy stock paper

glassine baggies
or paper bags

kraft paper

package tags

business cards (collected
from local businesses)

8 x 10-inch mailing envelope

ribbon

take-out menus (collected
from nearby restaurants)

magazines (to cut
photographs out of)

pens/markers

red electrical tape

brads

notebook paper

small picture frame

old belt

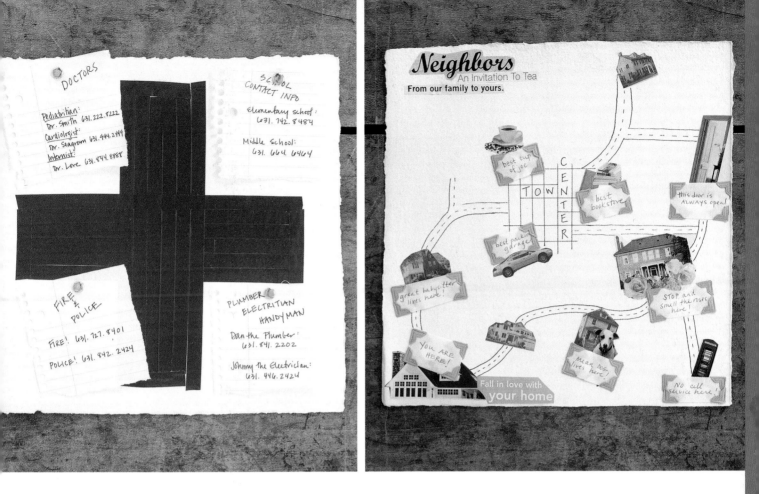

1. Using a straightedge, tear your paper to the size of your wooden boards.

2. Make as many pages as you'd like. Here are some suggestions for useful items to include:

NEIGHBORHOOD MAP: Draw a map of your neighborhood. Cut photos of houses out of magazines and paste them on the map to denote the different houses on the block. Indicate landmarks by hand writing small tags noting where the mean dog lives, where the sweet roses are, where the best neighborhood babysitter can be found, and so on.

BUSINESS CARDS: Cut some little glassine bags (or tiny brown paper bags) in half, glue each pocket to a rectangle of kraft paper, and glue the rectangles to your scrapbook page. Label each pocket with a packing tag according to the category — for example, fashion, services, home and garden, etc. Sort the cards you've gathered and insert them in the appropriate pockets.

TAKE-OUT MENUS: Cut off the flap of the mailing envelope. Punch two holes vertically on either side of the envelope and thread the ribbon through. Tie the ends of the ribbon in a small knot. Place the menus inside.

EMERGENCY: Use the electrical tape to make a red plus sign, dividing a scrapbook page into four sections. Within each section, use a brad to clip in a piece of notebook paper listing phone numbers of, for example, doctors, the fire department, the plumber, the children's school, etc.

3. Take a photo of your new neighbor's house, place it in the picture frame, and attach it to one of the wooden panels.

4. Write the family's name on a piece of paper and glue it under the photo of the house.

5. Arrange the scrapbook pages between the wooden panels and fasten the belt around your "guide."

SERVES 8

INGREDIENTS

4 tablespoons olive oil

2 onions, chopped

2 cloves garlic, minced

6 carrots, grated

2 pounds lean ground beef

2 cups ketchup

4 tablespoon molasses

1 tablespoon chili powder

1 tablespoon Worcestershire sauce

salt and pepper to taste

4 cups cheddar cheese, grated

2 tablespoons melted butter

1 package of premade dinner-roll dough

sesame seeds

1. Preheat oven to 375 degrees. In a large skillet, heat oil and sauté onions, garlic, and carrots until soft.

2. Add ground beef and cook until browned. Stir in ketchup, molasses, chili powder, and Worcestershire sauce. Season with salt and pepper to taste.

3. Gently simmer for 15 minutes. Remove from stove, transfer to a 3-quart casserole dish, and sprinkle with cheese.

4. Separate dinner-roll dough and place on top of cheese to cover casserole. Brush rolls with some melted butter and sprinkle with sesame seeds. Bake uncovered until rolls are golden brown, about 25 minutes.

Sloppy Joe Casserole

It is both my personal and professional opinion that when the chips are down nothing makes you feel better than some good old-fashioned comfort food. So after you have spent Saturday organizing the gang and preparing your traveling basket, spend Sunday in the kitchen mixing up some old-time family favorites. In the following recipes, I have put some new twists on the standard casserole. Not only do they travel well, but they can also be prepared ahead and heated later — perfect for a dinner on the move.

Spinach
Casserole

SERVES 6–8

INGREDIENTS

2 cups sour cream

2 envelopes onion soup mix

4 10-ounce packages whole-leaf or chopped
frozen spinach, thawed and drained well

1. Preheat oven to 350 degrees.

2. In a large bowl, combine sour cream
and onion soup mix. Add spinach and mix
together well.

3. Transfer to a 2-quart baking dish and
bake for 30 minutes, uncovered.

Shrimp
& Cheese Casserole

SERVES 8

INGREDIENTS

6 slices whole wheat bread

$1/2$ pound cheddar cheese

1 pound cooked shrimp

$1/4$ cup melted butter

3 eggs, beaten

$1/2$ teaspoon dry mustard

salt and pepper

1 pint milk

1. Break bread into quarter-inch pieces. Cut cheese into bite-size pieces.

2. Arrange bread, shrimp, and cheese in several layers in a 3-quart baking dish.

3. Pour melted butter over the layers.

4. Beat eggs. Add mustard, salt, pepper, and milk. Mix together and pour over shrimp layers. Cover and let stand for a minimum of 3 hours or overnight.

5. Preheat oven to 350 degrees. Bake for 1 hour, covered.

Potatoes Deluxe
Casserole

SERVES 8

INGREDIENTS

5 cups cooked frozen, diced potatoes (hash browns)

$1^1/2$ cups cottage cheese

$1^1/2$ cups sour cream

$1/2$ cup chopped onion

$1^1/2$ cups shredded cheddar cheese

4 tablespoons chopped chives

1 teaspoon salt

1. Preheat oven to 350 degrees.

2. Combine all ingredients in a 3-quart baking dish.

3. Bake for 1 hour.

English Apple Casserole

INGREDIENTS

5–8 tart apples, cored and sliced, skin left on

1 tablespoon cinnamon

1 teaspoon salt

1½ cups flour

1 cup sugar

¾ cup butter

1. Preheat oven to 400 degrees.

2. Sprinkle cinnamon and salt over apple slices and toss together. Place mixture in a 3-quart baking dish.

3. Combine flour, sugar, and butter to form crumbs. Spread over the apple mixture.

4. Bake for 10 minutes, then lower temperature to 350 degrees and bake for another 30 minutes or so.

5. Broil for about 5 minutes to brown top of casserole.

Strawberry Shortcake Casserole

SERVES 8

INGREDIENTS

1 day-old loaf of French bread

1 20-ounce bag frozen strawberries

6 ounces cream cheese

4 eggs

$^1/_2$ cup sour cream

2 teaspoons vanilla extract

$^1/_3$ cup brown sugar

$^2/_3$ cup white sugar

$^1/_4$ cup milk

1. Tear the bread into bite-size pieces. Place half the bread in a shallow, greased 2-quart baking dish. Sprinkle half of the strawberries over the bread.

2. In a mixing bowl, beat cream cheese until smooth. Beat in eggs, sour cream, and vanilla. Gradually beat in brown sugar, white sugar, and milk until blended.

3. Pour cream-cheese mixture over bread and strawberries. Cover and refrigerate for a few hours or overnight.

4. Preheat oven to 350 degrees.

5. Remove the casserole from refrigerator and let return to room temperature. Top with remaining half bag of strawberries.

6. Cover with foil and bake for 30 minutes. Uncover and bake for 20 minutes longer. When a knife inserted into the middle comes out clean, the casserole is done.

Often when I was in a bad mood, my mother would tell me to think of a Christmas tree, and when I was a young girl this worked quite well. Visions of walking into my living room on Christmas morning, seeing all the gifts—some wrapped with big bows and shiny paper, some right in plain sight ready to be touched and tested—oh, how my imagination would soar and, for a brief moment, allow me to be transported to the morning of December 25. As the images faded, my smile would remain; my mom's suggestion worked. However, now that I'm a grown-up, dreamy remedies such as these are not a sure thing. I need something a bit more tangible, a bit more long lasting. . . . Sure, a giant sundae, a new dress, a glass of champagne can all help, but, for various reasons, these all have their drawbacks. As an adult, I have had to find new ways to improve my outlook on life. . . a kind of emotional makeover, if you will.

When I was a rookie caterer in Los Angeles and could barely afford the groceries to prepare the meal I had promised, let alone flowers and decorations to set the mood, I found my solution. You see, I discovered a way to cut corners in order to afford my catering goals: a simple visit to the downtown flower mart and the farmers' market. I could not believe what a glorious way it was to start the day. I would begin my adventure early in the morning, before the city had begun to awaken. The flower wranglers, as I called them, would already be at their stands, prepared for the rush of florists, wedding planners, and caterers collecting their stems. Rows and aisles were filled with bright pinks, reds, yellows, and oranges. And the smells . . . I tell you, it could turn anyone's frown upside down. The farmers' market stands were equally as delightful . . . grand veggies and green herbs aplenty.

As I arranged, prepared, displayed, and enjoyed my garden treasures, all worries seemed trivial. I had found my adult therapy in these items from the earth . . . the perfection of a flower, the sweetness of a tomato, and the whiff of fresh mint all washed my troubles away. With a weekend spent immersed in recipes and projects inspired by the garden, I assure you, these earthly treasures can be any grown-up's Christmas tree.

find your green thumb

SECRET GARDEN

FLOWER POWER

Flower power — the following recipes and projects possess a lot of it! With every petal, whether freshly grown or artificial, these garden delights will cheer up any dreary decor or table. Have fun!

Garden Waters

Sure, on a summer day, you want your drinks to be refreshing. But doesn't it make it so much sweeter if they're also eye-catching? (See photo on page 42.)

SERVES 8

Lemon Herb Water

INGREDIENTS

2 lemons, sliced

1 bunch mint or basil

yellow or white rose petals

Combine lemon slices, mint or basil, and rose petals in a pitcher filled with icy water. Chill for 1–2 hours.

Berry Rose Water

INGREDIENTS

1 pint raspberries, fresh or frozen

pink rose petals

Combine raspberries and rose petals in a pitcher filled with icy water. Chill for 1–2 hours.

Orange Flower Water

INGREDIENTS

1 orange, sliced

nasturtiums

Combine orange slices and nasturtium petals in a pitcher filled with icy water. Chill for 1–2 hours.

RULE OF THUMB When cooking with flowers, always use pesticide-free.

Rosy Fudge

My stepgrandmother, Gladys Hyatt, used to make this for us every Christmas. Now I carry on the tradition. I must admit, it's just as good, but not as pretty, without the rose petals.

SERVES 8–10

INGREDIENTS

3 cups sugar

$3/4$ cup butter

$2/3$ cup evaporated milk

1 12-ounce package semisweet chocolate pieces

1 7-ounce jar marshmallow creme

1 cup chopped nuts

1 teaspoon vanilla extract

2 tablespoons rose (or other edible flower) petals torn into small pieces

1. Combine sugar, butter, and evaporated milk in a heavy 2 $1/2$-quart saucepan. Bring to a boil, stirring constantly. Continue boiling for 8–10 minutes over medium heat, stirring constantly to prevent scorching (sugar should reach softball stage).

2. Remove from heat. Stir in chocolate pieces until melted. Add marshmallow creme, nuts, and vanilla. Whisk until well blended.

3. Pour mixture into a greased 13-by-9-inch pan. Sprinkle rose petals over top and gently press into fudge. Cool at room temperature.

SERVES 8

INGREDIENTS

2 cups flour

1 1/2 teaspoons baking powder

1/4 teaspoon baking soda

1/4 teaspoon salt

12 tablespoons (1 1/2 sticks) unsalted butter, softened

1 1/2 cups sugar

3 large eggs

1 tablespoon chopped fresh thyme

2 teaspoons lemon peel, finely shredded

1/4 cup lemon juice

1 cup milk

1 cup sliced almonds

lavender-lemon glaze (see recipe at right)

sugared flowers (see recipe at right)

1. Preheat oven to 350 degrees.

2. Grease and lightly flour a 9 x 5 x 3-inch loaf pan. Set aside.

3. In a bowl, sift together flour, baking powder, baking soda, and salt. Set aside.

4. In a large bowl, using a mixer, beat butter on high speed for 30 seconds. Add sugar and beat until light and fluffy, about 5 minutes.

5. Add eggs, one at a time, beating well after each addition.

6. In a small bowl, mix thyme, lemon peel, lemon juice, and milk. Stir to combine. (Mixture may appear curdled.)

7. On low speed, alternately add flour mixture and milk mixture to the butter-and-sugar mixture. Mix each addition until just combined.

8. Fold in almonds.

9. Pour batter into the loaf pan. Bake for about 60 minutes, or until a toothpick comes out clean when inserted into the middle. Let cool for 15 minutes.

Lavender-Lemon Glaze

INGREDIENTS

1–2 tablespoons lavender

1/2 cup sugar

3/4 cup lemon juice

1. In a food processor, blend lavender flowers with sugar.

2. Stir together lemon juice and sugar in a small saucepan. Bring to a boil. Reduce heat and simmer uncovered for 10 minutes, or until sugar has dissolved and mixture is slightly thickened. Stir occasionally.

3. Brush glaze immediately onto cake.

Sugared Flowers

INGREDIENTS

6–12 edible flowers

2–3 egg whites

sugar for sprinkling

1. Dip flowers in egg whites or brush egg whites onto flower petals. Sprinkle lightly with sugar.

2. Place on a baking sheet to dry and crystallize.

3. Decorate top of cake with flowers.

Lemon-Thyme
Pound Cake with Sugared Petals

This is a fancy, girly, springy flowering treat.

Sometimes it can make even more of an impact if you place a single flower in a contrasting large vase. It not only pleases the eye, it pleases the pocketbook!

TOOLS
flower cutters

MATERIALS
fresh-cut flowers
large wide-mouth glass
containers or vases

1. Take a single-stemmed flower with a large bloom or multiple large blooms and remove a majority or all of the leaves.

2. Cut the stem on an angle (this will help the flower last longer).

3. Angle the single stem in a wide-mouth container or vase.

Big & Tall

"Think outside the box" or "think inside the vase," as the case may be. Sometimes a simple, singular flower can pack a big punch.

Think Inside the Vase

TOOLS
flower cutters

MATERIALS
glass containers and vases
fresh-cut flowers

Jam Jar
Fill jar approximately half full with water, float a flower head, and seal.

Candy Jar
Fill jar approximately a quarter full with water, float a flower head, and cover.

A Vase within a Vase
Fill tiny bud vase with water, place a single-stemmed flower inside, and cover with larger vase by turning it upside down and over the top of the smaller vase.

Picasso's Petunias
& Mums by Monet

Have you ever looked at a flower and thought, "How can this beautiful thing come from the earth?" Now you can give your flowers their due respect and display them in your home as the works of art that they truly are.

OPTION #1

MATERIALS

photo clips

mat cutouts

clear marbles

small vases

fresh-cut flowers

1. Using a stand-up photo clip, clip on your mat vertically.

2. Secure the base of the clips inside a small vase with glass marbles.

3. Place a flower stem among the marbles, fill the vase with water, and let the flower peek through the opening of the mat.

OPTION #2

TOOLS

hot-glue gun

MATERIALS

frame with fitted mat

empty box whose length is equal to or less than the width of the frame

fresh-cut flowers

small vases

clear marbles

1. Remove glass from frame and glue mat to the inside edge.

2. Hot-glue the long side of the box to the bottom back of the frame.

3. Insert flowers into small glass vases, use marbles to secure stems, fill with water, and place the vases in the box behind the frame.

4. Cut the stems so that the flowers peek through the openings in the frame.

Hoop It Up!

When I say you'll need fabric and embroidery hoops for this project, you think you'll need to know how to sew, right? Wrong! This is the solution for you if you're looking for a bold and inexpensive way to decorate a wall and you want to keep the mood-altering image of flowers around longer than they would last in a vase.

TOOLS
fabric scissors
hammer

MATERIALS
embroidery hoops
in different sizes
floral fabrics
glue
large-head nails

1. Lay a hoop on top of the part of the fabric that you want to show off.

2. Cut the fabric around the hoop about ½ inch wider than the embroidery circle.

3. Separate the two sides of the embroidery hoop and secure the fabric in the center, pulling it tight enough to keep the fabric from bowing in the middle.

4. Glue the edge of the fabric to the inside of the inner hoop.

5. Hammer a nail into your wall and hang the hoop on it.

THE BIG IDEA Working in multiples is a great design technique, so for this project we suggest you do a grouping of several hoops on one wall.

VEGETABLE PATCH

A vegetable patch is one of my very favorite sights, but "eat your vegetables" has always been one of my least favorite orders. I can guarantee that these recipes will make you want to dig into the greens. And if I simply can't convince you to eat your veggies, perhaps I can entice you to use these green dreams in a fun, indulgent way.

Cool as a Cucumber!

Computer screens, televisions, business documents —all things that make our eyes and heads sore and tired. Ease your tired eyes just before bedtime with this simple, relaxing toner, and in the morning you will be that wide-eyed, well-rested self you know and love! (See photo on page 54.)

TOOLS

blender

sieve

chopping knife

MATERIALS

1 fresh cucumber to yield $1/4$ cup juice (see directions)

2 tablespoons witch hazel

2 tablespoons distilled water

clean clear bottle

decorative tag

twine

1. Prepare the cucumber juice by chopping up the cucumber (peel and all) and liquefying it in the blender. Using the sieve, strain off the clear green juice. Discard the pulp.

2. Mix the clear green juice together with the remainder of the ingredients.

3. Pour the liquid into bottle and close lid tightly. Embellish the bottle with a tag and twine wrapped around the neck.

BASIC 1-2-3 Store your toner in the refrigerator so it will last longer and have a cold, tingling effect.

Pickled Veggies

This is one of my favorite things to make when my vegetable drawer is full of veggies that are just about to spoil. It's a great way to rescue them and enjoy them later. When refrigerated, these little gems will last up to a week and a half.

SERVES 4

INGREDIENTS

1 cup white wine vinegar

$1/4$ cup water

3 tablespoons sugar

2 teaspoons salt

2 teaspoons whole coriander seeds

1 teaspoon whole mustard seeds

$1/4$ teaspoon red chili flakes

2 cucumbers, sliced or cut into spears — or any other vegetable, such as carrots, green beans, radishes, etc.

1. Combine vinegar, water, sugar, salt, coriander, mustard seeds, and red chili flakes in a small saucepan and bring to a boil. Cook until the sugar has dissolved. Remove from heat and let cool for 5 minutes.

2. Place cucumbers or other vegetables in a medium bowl or jar. Pour the vinegar mixture over. Cover and refrigerate for at least 1 hour before serving.

Harvest Bread Pudding

The Zucchini. This recipe will convert
even a zucchini skeptic into a fan.

SERVES 8

INGREDIENTS

2 tablespoons olive oil

1 zucchini, sliced $1/4$-inch thick

1 yellow squash, sliced $1/4$-inch thick

$1/2$ cup frozen corn

1 tablespoon minced garlic

1 tablespoon chopped fresh basil

1 tablespoon chopped fresh parsley

1 tablespoon chopped fresh sage

5 cups cubed sourdough bread

1 cup shredded Swiss cheese

3 tablespoons chopped pecans

2 cups half-and-half

5 eggs, slightly beaten

salt and pepper

1. Preheat oven to 350 degrees.

2. Grease a 2-quart baking dish and set aside.

3. In a skillet, heat olive oil and cook zucchini, squash, and corn over medium heat for about 3 minutes. Stir in garlic and herbs. Cook until zucchini and squash are tender, about 2–3 more minutes.

4. Remove from heat and stir in bread cubes.

5. Place half of the mixture in the prepared baking dish. Sprinkle half of the Swiss cheese on top. Cover that with the rest of the mixture and sprinkle with the remainder of the cheese and the nuts.

6. In a bowl, whisk together the half-and-half, eggs, and salt and pepper to taste. Pour over bread mixture.

7. Bake uncovered for 35 minutes, or until a knife inserted in the middle comes out clean. Let stand and cool for 10 minutes.

I live in the Hamptons, where fresh tomatoes are grown in abundance, so I'm always looking for new ways to serve these bright-red delectables.

Simple Baked
Tomatoes

SERVES 4

INGREDIENTS

4 ripe beefsteak tomatoes

1 cup breadcrumbs

6 tablespoons olive oil

1 tablespoon chopped fresh basil

1 tablespoon chopped fresh parsley

1 tablespoon chopped fresh rosemary

1 tablespoon chopped fresh thyme

salt and pepper

1. Preheat oven to 350 degrees.
2. Slice tomatoes in half. Place each half, cut side up, on a cookie sheet.
3. In a small bowl, mix breadcrumbs, olive oil, and fresh herbs.
4. Season tomatoes with salt and pepper. Place breadcrumb mix on top of tomatoes.
5. Bake until tomatoes are heated through and breadcrumb mixture is toasted.

Salmon & Spinach

Rolled in a Puff Pastry

SERVED WITH HOLLANDAISE

I love an all-in-one dish!

SERVES 8–10

Salmon & Spinach Roll

INGREDIENTS

1 package puff pastry (2 sheets)

1 tablespoon fresh parsley, chopped

1 tablespoon fresh thyme, chopped

4 tablespoons butter

$1/2$ shallot, chopped

$1^1/_2$ cups frozen chopped spinach, thawed and drained

3 8-ounce salmon filets, diced

salt and pepper

olive oil

1. Preheat oven to 350 degrees.

2. Put 2 sheets of puff pastry on top of each other. Roll out puff pastry on a lightly floured surface into a rectangle approximately 12 by 15 inches. Sprinkle with parsley, thyme, salt, and pepper.

3. In a sauté pan, melt 2 tablespoons of butter and sauté the shallots until translucent. Add spinach and sauté for 3 minutes. Remove from heat and cool mixture.

4. Spread spinach over pastry, top with diced salmon, and season with salt and pepper.

5. Roll up pastry, tucking ends in as you roll. Wrap pastry in parchment paper buttered with 2 table-spoons of butter and tie it up with kitchen string to hold roll together. Rub outside of paper with olive oil. Place on a baking sheet and bake for 45 minutes.

6. Unwrap, slice roll, and serve with dill hollandaise. (see recipe at right).

Dill Hollandaise

INGREDIENTS

3 egg yolks

salt and pepper

1–2 tablespoons lemon juice

2 sticks unsalted butter

dill, snipped

1. In a blender, combine egg yolks, pepper, and 1 tablespoon of lemon juice.

2. In a small saucepan, melt the butter and heat until bubbling hot.

3. Cover the blender and blend the egg yolk mixture on high speed for several seconds.

4. Either remove center cap of blender lid or carefully remove lid itself with blender still running.

5. Pour hot butter in a thin stream into whirring egg mixture.

6. Add dill and pulse to combine.

7. Taste sauce and adjust seasoning with lemon juice, salt, and pepper.

BASIC 1-2-3 If sauce gets too thick, add one table-spoon of hot water at a time to make it thinner.

HERB DELIGHT

When I was a struggling actress in Los Angeles, the thing that lifted my spirits was the bed of mint outside the window of my dingy studio apartment. The wind would blow, and the smell of the mint would come wafting in. Ahhh…all was well. As you take in the scents, textures, and beauty of the herbs in your secret garden, I hope your troubles will seem less worrisome.

Potpourri
of Herb Salad

When I was growing up in northern Michigan, it seemed as if everyone and their uncle had an herb garden. The bounty of herbs delivered to our home was constant. And one of our favorite ways to enjoy them was mixed with a light, lemony dressing.

SERVES 8

INGREDIENTS

1 lemon, zest and juice

salt and pepper

$1/4$ cup olive oil

$1/2$ cup fresh parsley leaves

$1/2$ cup fresh mint leaves

$1/2$ cup fresh basil leaves

$1/4$ cup fresh chives

$1/2$ cup fresh chervil

2 sprigs fresh tarragon leaves

1. In a bowl, whisk together lemon zest, lemon juice, and salt and pepper to taste. While whisking, drizzle in olive oil.

2. In a large bowl, toss herbs together with the dressing. Season with salt and pepper to taste.

Curried Chicken, Walnut, & Grape Salad

I got this recipe from my friend Diane, who is an exotic gourmet cook. This is probably the easiest recipe she has and the only one I could re-create. But don't let its simplicity fool you — it tastes as though it comes from an expert's kitchen.

SERVES 4

INGREDIENTS

$3/4$ cup mayonnaise

2 tablespoons curry powder

2 tablespoons lemon juice

4 cups shredded poached chicken (about 4–6 breasts)

1 cup seedless red grapes, sliced in half

$1/2$ cup chopped walnuts

$1/2$ cup chopped parsley

salt and pepper

lettuce or carrots for garnish

In a large bowl, combine mayonnaise, curry powder, and lemon juice. Mix in chicken, grapes, walnuts, and parsley. Season with salt and pepper to taste. Serve on a bed of lettuce or sautéed julienne carrots.

Classic Basil Pesto

INGREDIENTS

2 cups fresh basil leaves

2 tablespoons pine nuts

1 clove garlic, smashed

1/3 cup olive oil

1/4 cup grated Parmesan cheese

salt and pepper

1. Place basil, pine nuts, garlic, and oil in a blender or food processor and blend until smooth. Add the cheese and blend a few seconds longer. Season with salt and pepper to taste.

YOU CAN'T GO WRONG Use this pesto on fresh pasta or swirl it into vegetable soup.

Cilantro Pesto

INGREDIENTS

2 cups chopped cilantro leaves

1 tablespoon pumpkin seeds

1 clove garlic, smashed

1/3 – 1/2 cup olive oil

salt and pepper

1. Place all ingredients in a blender or food processor and blend until smooth. Season with salt and pepper.

YOU CAN'T GO WRONG Try this with chicken or pork.

Mint Pesto

INGREDIENTS

1 cup loosely packed fresh mint leaves

1 cup loosely packed fresh flat-leaf parsley

2 tablespoons blanched almonds, toasted and chopped

1 clove garlic, smashed

1/3 – 1/2 cup olive oil

salt and pepper

1. Place all ingredients in a blender or food processor and blend until smooth. Season with salt and pepper.

YOU CAN'T GO WRONG Serve this with lamb.

Trio of Zesty Pestos

Once you see how easy it is to invent and create your own combinations of pesto, you'll probably never want to buy it from the store again.

SERVES 4

Marinated Feta Cheese

This is a great way to make a great cheese greater.

SERVES 6–8

INGREDIENTS

1 cup fresh feta cheese, cut into large cubes

2 cups olive oil

2 cut-up garlic cloves

3–4 sprigs fresh rosemary

1 teaspoon multicolored peppercorns

1 teaspoon chili flakes

1. Combine most of the oil and the garlic, rosemary, peppercorns, and chili flakes in a large bowl.

2. Add feta cheese.

3. Add more olive oil to completely cover cheese. Marinate for 1 hour at room temperature.

Spiced Goat Cheese

I've been accused of being a goat cheese addict, but if I dress it up with a plethora of herbs, nobody knows that I am again indulging in one of my favorite snacks.

SERVES 6–8

INGREDIENTS

goat cheese log or goat cheese rolled into balls
mixture of fresh rosemary, thyme, and marjoram, finely chopped

Roll the goat cheese log or balls in herb mixture until coated.

YES YOU CAN You can also make this with dried herbs.

Parmesan Wafers

You won't want to bite into these because they are so beautiful. But you will soooo be missing out because they are sooooo tasty!

INGREDIENTS

¾ cup coarsely grated Parmesan cheese

fresh tarragon

fresh basil

fresh chervil

fresh sage

1. Preheat oven to 350 degrees.

2. Spoon grated Parmesan onto a cookie sheet in 1–2-teaspoon-size mounds about 2 inches apart. Push down on the Parmesan mounds with the back of a spoon to slightly spread out the cheese.

3. Place an herb sprig on top of each Parmesan mound.

4. Bake until melted and golden (about 3–4 minutes).

Store-Bought Surprises

I believe in cheating . . . in the kitchen, that is.
Why not take advantage of modern food science
and use prepared items that you can dress up
to make your own?

SERVES 6–8

Herbed Sugar Cookies

INGREDIENTS

1 package store-bought sugar-cookie dough

fresh herbs, snipped

sugar

1. Preheat oven to 350 degrees.

2. Slice cookie dough according to directions on package.

3. Lay herbs flat and slightly press them down into cookie dough.

4. Sprinkle cookies with sugar.

5. Bake according to package instructions.

Pesto Biscuits

INGREDIENTS

1 package prepared biscuit dough

store-bought pesto

1. Cut each premade biscuit in half.

2. Spread bottom half with pesto and top with other half.

3. Bake as directed on package.

Croissant Herb Roll Ups

INGREDIENTS

1 package store-bought croissant dough

1 tablespoon mustard

3 tablespoons fresh herbs, snipped

2 tablespoons butter, melted

1. Preheat oven to 350 degrees.

2. Unroll croissant dough onto a cookie sheet.

3. Brush a thin layer of mustard onto dough and sprinkle with fresh herbs.

4. Roll up dough into a croissant

5. Brush croissant with melted butter.

6. Bake according to package instructions.

It's the weekend, and a warm bath is calling your name! Here is a fantastic homemade treat that you can mix up in the kitchen and enjoy in the bathroom. Drop this fizzy bath bomb in your tub and let the scent of wildflowers take you to your own secret garden.

TOOLS

large bowl

sieve

small bowl

MATERIALS

1½ cups baking soda

½ cup citric acid powder

2 teaspoons rose oil

food coloring

plastic ball molds

ivy leaves

twine

1. In large bowl, sift together baking soda and citric acid powder.

2. In small bowl, mix together almond extract and 6 drops of food coloring

3. Pour the wet mixture (½ teaspoon at a time) into the dry ingredients (½ cup at a time) and stir quickly, before it starts to fizz.

4. Wipe a little rose oil into each mold to prevent sticking. Fill the molds with the mixture, packing it in firmly to create a smooth ball shape. Let the mixture harden in the mold for 24 hours, then remove.

5. Wrap an ivy leaf around the ball and secure it with twine.

Have a Ball in the Bath!

TOOLS
drill

MATERIALS
charcoal

all-mount plant rings

pots

herbs

1. Sketch out on a small piece of paper the way you want your vines to look.

2. Using a thick piece of charcoal, draw your vines on the wall. Draw a few leaves and some extra curlicues.

3. With the given hardware, mount your plant rings onto the wall using the drill, positioning them along the sprouting branches you've drawn.

4. Plant your favorite herbs in the pots and rest them in the plant rings.

YOU CAN'T GO WRONG Find studs as a guide for where the pots are going to hang.

Wallflower

It's your house and you can draw on the wall if you want to! While you're at it, why not turn your drawing into a live herb garden? It can double as a dreamy indoor garden while bearing fresh herbs that no one can resist!

AROUND

As you know, I am from a small town in the Midwest. There, it was considered gourmet if we had fresh iceberg lettuce in our fridge . . . there was no such thing as baby veggies, mixed greens, or heirloom tomatoes. My father insists that the test of a true chef is whether he or she can cook a good steak or bake a good chocolate chip cookie. He has no admiration for the subtlety of a French sauce, the delicacy of homemade pasta, or the intricacies of eastern spices. You get what I'm saying . . . meat and potatoes were all the rage growing up.

I learned a lot about basic cooking from my mother, my aunts, and their friends, and for that I am eternally grateful. As they say, *real food for real people.*

I left the simple kitchens of my youth to find an entire world of culinary flavors: I worked as a waitress and spent all my time in restaurant kitchens trying to soak up the habits of the more worldly chefs; I bought books that highlighted cooking from around the globe; and I dined at restaurants in my new cosmopolitan home that introduced me to all sorts of new tastes.

Slowly but surely, I started introducing more and more of these exotic ingredients into my cooking repertoire. By the time I started my own catering company, my cuisine was based in my midwestern roots but had a foot in the tastes from around the world.

If you, the "chefs" of your family, or your friends are stuck in a cooking rut just like my midwestern family, then how about spending an entire weekend taking your family on a culinary jaunt around the world? Throughout the following projects and recipes you will find ideas that evoke the art, colors, and customs of many cultures. In these recipes you will find easy ways to incorporate new scents, tastes, and textures that are sure to liven up your nightly dining habits.

exotic travel without leaving home

THE WORLD

MEXICAN

My sister Marlee is an artist who recently bought a home in the very creative community of San Miguel, Mexico. She sends me treats from her faraway location, the most recent being a Christmas manger set, handcrafted by local artists. The deep red colors and the earthy tones of the figures are some of the many reasons I cannot wait to visit there. But until my ticket is booked, I will have to settle my curiosity about the local art through this place mat project. The hay-filled centerpiece was inspired by the feel of the country. These creations accompany a menu that incorporates the flavors of my sister's newfound country. So come join me in an art-inspired fiesta!

Pomegranates
in a Haystack

Beauty can be found in the most unpredictable places. This centerpiece will whisk you south of the border with its rustic, natural appeal and its contrasting colors and textures.

MATERIALS

clear plastic or glass container

hay

6 pomegranates

1.   **Fill your container about ³/₄ of the way with hay.**

2.   **Place your pomegranates throughout the hay and set the container in the middle of the table.**

MAKE IT CHIC This project is a perfect reason to bring that old fish tank out of the basement and onto your lunch table!

Mats of Mexico

As an art history major, I love this project because it encourages you to investigate the art of the region. Start a dinner-table discussion about the art you've featured in these place mats.

TOOLS

computer

scissors

MATERIALS

Latin American art prints

8¹/₂-by-11-inch sheets of photo paper

11-by-14-inch float frames

double-sided tape

red ribbon

1.   **Scan the prints into your computer and print out a full-frame reproduction onto photo paper. (Or use prints that are about 8½ x 11".)**

2.   **Center the colorful art print onto the sheet of your float frame. Hold it down with double-sided tape.**

3.   **Cut 2 11-inch pieces and 2 14-inch pieces of ribbon for each mat. Make a diagonal cut at the end of each ribbon so that they will neatly match up in the corners of the float frame. Hold the ribbon down with double-sided tape.**

4.   **Cover with the top sheet of glass or Plexiglas from the frame and attach with the hardware provided.**

YES, YOU CAN Find colorful Mexican art images on the Internet, or use photos from an old art book or calendar. Works by such artists as Frida Kahlo, Diego Rivera, Guillermo Trujillo, and Rufino Tamayo are all great choices.

INGREDIENTS

1 15-ounce can whole tomatoes

1 onion, chopped

4 cloves garlic, minced

1 chipotle pepper, seeded

1 48-ounce can chicken broth

salt and pepper

corn tortillas, cut into $\frac{1}{4}$-inch strips

olive oil for frying

juice of 1 lime

Sopa de Tortilla

This soup is one of my favorites because it brings back fond memories of my kind friend Kerstin, who cooked for me when I was on bed rest while expecting my first child.

1. In a blender or food processor, puree the tomatoes, onion, garlic, and chipotle pepper.

2. In a large pot, combine the tomato mixture with the chicken broth. Bring to a boil and simmer. Season with salt and pepper.

3. Fill a frying pan a quarter of the way up with oil. Heat the oil and fry the tortilla strips until they are crispy and golden. Remove them from the oil and sprinkle with salt.

4. Remove the soup from the heat and add the lime juice.

5. Garnish each serving with fried tortilla strips.

MAKE IT CHIC This soup also tastes and looks great when you add some diced avocado, thinly sliced green onion, sour cream, grated cheese, chopped cilantro, and lime wedges.

INGREDIENTS

2 pounds cod

1 tablespoon chili powder

2 teaspoons brown sugar

1/2 teaspoon each salt and pepper

olive oil for sautéing

1 cup salsa

juice of 2 limes

1/2 can black beans, rinsed and drained

2 green onions, thinly sliced

1/4 cup chopped cilantro

1 avocado, pitted and diced

corn tortillas

3 cups shredded lettuce

sour cream (optional)

1.   Rinse the fish and pat it dry. Set aside.

2.   In a bowl, combine the chili powder, brown sugar, and 1/2 tsp. each of salt and pepper. Rub the mixture into the fish on both sides.

3.   Heat a little oil in a large skillet. Sauté the fish until it flakes easily. Remove from heat. Break the fish into large chunks.

4.   In a bowl, combine the salsa, lime juice, black beans, green onions, cilantro, and avocado.

5.   Warm the tortillas in the oven or on the stovetop over a low flame.

6.   Divide the fish and the bean mixture equally among the tortillas. Top with lettuce and, if desired, sour cream.

Spicy Avocado, Fish,
& Black Bean Taco Salad

This recipe is my attempt at re-creating the fish taco at Benito's taco shop, near my old store in Los Angeles. I spent many a lunch hour going through their car wash while munching on a delicious taco to go! I think this more elegant salad does Benito's justice.

Zingy Limeade

This recipe is a variation on family punch called Giggle Juice that always whets my appetite on summer days. I find this south of the border rendition equally thirst-quenching and festive, especially if you dip the top of the glasses in water and then coat them with sugar, creating a sweet rim on top of the sour juice. Olé!

SERVES 4

INGREDIENTS

1 can frozen limeade concentrate
1 bottle club soda, or seltzer
mint sprigs

1. Prepare limeade according to the directions on the can, substituting club soda for water.

2. Add mint sprigs. Chill before serving.

MOROCCAN

Do you ever feel uncool, out of step, not hip? If you do, I advise an exploration of all things Moroccan. Enjoy the colors, the spices, the textiles, and the flavors. Complete immersion will help anybody get their groove back!

Golden Starry
Table Tiles

Spice up the center of your Moroccan dinner party with this golden, glittery table runner that is reminiscent of traditional Moroccan tile decor.

TOOLS

paintbrush

scissors

hammer

hot-glue gun

MATERIALS

4–6 square, thick wooden blocks, about 12 x 12"

2-inch-wide sparkly ribbon

brass upholstery tacks

Moroccan-style ornaments

deep orange paint

1. Paint your wooden blocks deep orange. Let dry overnight.

2. Lay your ribbon across the top and down the sides of each block. Cut the ribbon so that the ends are tucked under the block. Cut another piece of ribbon the same length; this can either lie parallel to the first ribbon or can cross over it to make a plus sign. Alternate these designs from block to block.

3. Attach the ribbon using your tacks. Leave about 1–2 inches in between each tack. Make sure to leave a space in the center with no upholstery tacks so that the ornament (step 4) will lie flat.

4. In the center of each block, hot-glue a Moroccan-style ornament.

Bejeweled Bundles

Dress up your napkins just like you would your wrist, with golden baubles that any Moroccan princess would envy!

MATERIALS

napkins

bangles

bendable jeweled ornaments

1. For half the napkins, gather each one in the center and slip 5–6 bangles over it.

2. For the other half, bend your ornaments into a cufflike shape and slide a napkin through each one.

3. Alternate your bangles and your cuffs every other place setting.

Cinnamon, Ginger,
& Cumin Lamb Stew

I love this recipe because it's oh-so-simple, and yet oh-so-exotic.

SERVES 6

INGREDIENTS

oil for sautéing

salt and pepper

3 pounds lamb, cubed

2 small onions, diced

1 leek, well cleaned and sliced thin
(white and light-green parts only)

3 cloves garlic, minced

1½ teaspoons cinnamon

1½ teaspoons cumin

1½ teaspoons ginger

6 ounces dates

3 ounces black olives, pitted

1 red bell pepper, diced

6 tablespoons chopped parsley

1 14½-ounce can stewed tomatoes

2 cups beef broth

1. In a large pot, heat about 1 tablespoon of the oil. Season the lamb with salt and pepper and brown it on all sides in the oil, working in batches. Transfer the lamb to a plate.

2. Add a little more oil to the pot if necessary. Sauté the onions and leek until softened. Add the garlic, cinnamon, cumin, ginger, dates, olives, bell pepper, parsley, and tomatoes and sauté for 1 minute. Add the lamb cubes and enough broth to cover, about 2 cups.

3. Cover the pot and simmer for 1 hour, until the lamb falls apart, adding more broth if necessary. Season with salt and pepper.

Spicy Vegetable
Couscous

Needless to say, I can cook a potato any which way. It wasn't until recently that I developed a palate for other side dishes and therefore a desire to find ways to make them my own. The following recipe is one of my favorite attempts.

SERVES 6

INGREDIENTS

1 box couscous

oil for sautéing

1 zucchini, diced

1 red onion, finely diced

1 teaspoon cumin

1 teaspoon turmeric

1 teaspoon red chili flakes

1 can chickpeas, drained and rinsed

1 green onion, thinly sliced

salt and pepper

1. Prepare the couscous according to package instructions.

2. Heat a little oil in a sauté pan. Add the zucchini and red onion along with the spices. Sauté until the zucchini is a little softened. Add the chickpeas and green onion and continue sautéing until the chickpeas are heated through.

3. Toss the vegetables with the couscous. Season with salt and pepper and toss again.

Orange, Mint, &
Red Onion Salad

Each year in the dead of winter, for Christmas, we would get a box of fresh oranges from my Uncle Bruce and Aunt Barb, delivered from Florida. I can't tell you how happy we were to see these citrus jewels. This is a great way to enhance their flavor and add a touch of breeziness to a heavy Moroccan supper.

SERVES 6

INGREDIENTS

1 teaspoon Dijon mustard

2 teaspoons honey

juice of 1 orange

1 tablespoon olive oil

salt and pepper

6 oranges, peeled and sliced

1 small red onion, thinly sliced

5 sprigs mint, chopped

1.   In a bowl, whisk together the mustard, honey, orange juice, and olive oil. Add salt and pepper to taste.

2.   In a shallow bowl, combine the orange slices, onion slices, and mint. Pour the dressing over the salad and toss.

3.   Let sit for 15 minutes before serving.

Brown-Sugared
Cantaloupe

When I was growing up, my mom ate cantaloupe for breakfast at least four times a week! And she would sprinkle it to death with salt because she swore it brought out more of the cantaloupe flavor. I'm not saying my mom is wrong, but I've found that this Moroccan method of baking it with spices is what truly brings it to life.

SERVES 6

INGREDIENTS

1 cantaloupe melon, peeled, halved, then each half cut into thirds

2 cups red wine

1 cup sugar

3 whole star anise

½ teaspoon cloves

½ teaspoon allspice

6 tablespoons brown sugar

1 tablespoon butter

1. Preheat the oven to 400 degrees.

2. Place the cantaloupe in a baking dish. Add the red wine, sugar, star anise, cloves, and allspice. Sprinkle with the brown sugar and dot with butter.

3. Bake until the brown sugar is melted, about 10–15 minutes. Remove the dish from the oven and transfer the cantaloupe to a serving dish.

4. In a saucepan, reduce the liquid until it is a thick syrup. Pour over the cantaloupe.

BASIC 1-2-3 Serve the melon over ice cream or topped with crème fraîche.

CHINESE

China is a place I always seem *so close* to visiting. My sisters and I had planned a trip there, but since my first television pilot was a success, I had to go into production immediately. Therefore, no trip to China.

My husband always said he was going to propose to me at the Great Wall of China, but instead, the big question was popped over dirty dishes on our dining table. You see, my infatuation with China began when I was a fifth-grader. My mother went there with an alumni group from the University of Michigan and came back with trinkets and tales that piqued my curiosity about this mysterious, exotic place. She brought us gifts that were extremely delicate and intricate in their design. I remember her talking about the creativity the Chinese possess when preparing food. She described one very memorable image of a tail of a peacock formed out of various dyed and sliced eggs. And then there was the new tapestry in our entry hall. My mother had purchased this spectacular fabric, embroidered with wildlife and flowers, and displayed it between two pieces of glass. I would sit and stare at that work of art for hours and dream of my very own trip to China. But still, no trip has occurred. Instead, I heat up my stove, prepare my own food, and set the stage for a Far East excursion for which I write my own fortune that says . . . yes, you guessed it . . . *You will be traveling to China shortly.*

Crack the Future

Predict the future for yourself and your lunch guests by making these delicate fortune eggs that are fun party favors!

TOOLS

pushpin or needle

scissors

pen

MATERIALS

eggs

paper

1. Punch a small hole with a pushpin or needle in the top and bottom of each egg and empty it of its contents. The best way to do this is to put your mouth to one of the holes and blow.

2. Cut your paper into 2-inch-long strips, write a fortune on each, fold it in half, and insert it into an egg.

HERE TO STAY You can find fortunes on the Internet, save them from past Chinese take-out, or write your own!

Boxed Garden

It is hard not to be amazed by the elegance of Chinese-language characters. The graceful lines impress us with their delicacy. Bring these beautiful characters into your Chinese lunch-table decor as a unique centerpiece, and I promise, the Far East really won't seem so *far* away! (See photo on page 96.)

TOOLS

scissors

paintbrush

MATERIALS

Chinese newspaper

double-sided tape

3 boxes, various sizes

high-gloss polyurethane

packing peanuts or newspaper

green moss

1. Cut sections from the Chinese newspaper and tape them to the surface of your boxes.

2. Create a border around the top edge of the boxes using larger type from the newspaper's headlines.

3. Coat the paper with polyurethane.

4. Fill each box to approximately one inch from the top with either packing peanuts or newspaper and cover the surface with green moss.

Plum-Glazed Ribs

One of my husband's favorite foods is ribs. He orders them from take-out at least twice a week, and I think when he was a bachelor, he ate them more like four times a week. However, when I was pregnant, I couldn't even have a rib in the same room with me. Now, I can once again enjoy my husband's obsession. And this is one of the best.

SERVES 4–6

INGREDIENTS

2 pounds pork ribs

1-inch-thick piece ginger, peeled and grated

2 cloves garlic, minced

2 tablespoons soy sauce

2 tablespoons sherry

2 tablespoons hoisin sauce

5 tablespoons plum sauce, plus extra for basting

salt and pepper

3 green onions, thinly sliced

1. Preheat the oven to 350 degrees.

2. Combine the ginger, garlic, soy sauce, sherry, hoisin sauce, plum sauce, and salt and pepper, and marinate the ribs in this mixture for at least half an hour.

3. Bake for 1 hour. Halfway through the cooking time, baste the meat with plum sauce and cover with foil to prevent the bones from getting burned. Top with the sliced green onions.

Sesame Noodles
WITH SCALLIONS AND SNOW PEAS

I used to cook food for a place in Los Angeles called Big and Tall Books. This was one of my favorite recipes to make, and one of my favorites for patrons to eat. Enjoy!

SERVES 4–6

INGREDIENTS

1 egg

2 egg yolks

2 tablespoons rice-wine vinegar

2 tablespoons soy sauce

3 tablespoons Dijon mustard

1/4 cup dark sesame oil

1/2 cup corn oil

1/2 pound linguine or other thin pasta

3–4 teaspoons chili oil

green onions, thinly sliced

1/4 pound snow peas, thinly sliced lengthwise

1.   Combine the first five ingredients in a blender.

2.   While the blender is on, add the sesame and corn oils in a slow, steady stream.

3.   Cook the pasta according to package instructions. Drain well and put into a large bowl. Dress the hot pasta with the sesame mayo.

4.   Add the chili oil, green onions, and snow peas. Toss to combine.

FRENCH

I studied in France for one year during my college years at Cornell, mostly because I wanted to learn the language. Toward the end of my stay there, I was shopping in a market when I asked in my best French the price of something. The annoyed proprietor rolled his eyes and responded to my question in his very best English. Oh, how sad I was that after much study I had not mastered the language well enough to pass as a French girl. Although I was defeated in the language department, I still take heart in my ability to travel back there by re-creating the charm of the French dining experience. Bon appétit!

Frenched
Tomatoes

This is a classic dish of my mother's. We thought it was so gourmet to have something called "Frenched" tomatoes, when it's actually one of the simplest recipes I know. But it does exemplify one of the things that French cuisine does best — highlight the natural flavors of foods without much fuss. (See photo on page 102.)

SERVES 6

INGREDIENTS

4 beefsteak tomatoes, thickly sliced

olive oil

2 teaspoons balsamic vinegar

4 tablespoons chopped parsley

salt and pepper

In a large bowl, combine the tomatoes, olive oil, balsamic vinegar, and parsley. Toss gently to combine. Season with salt and pepper to taste.

Couture of **Provence**

There's nothing better than French couture — so why not bring it to your table by designing your own line of place mats?

TOOLS
scissors

MATERIALS
blue-and-white fabric

scrap paper

bias tape

fabric glue

Like any true designer, you'll want to be creative with your place mat shape. You could cut each one differently or cut a pattern freehand. But if you need some guidance, follow these steps.

1.   Cut a piece of paper measuring 12 x 14 inches. Fold it in half lengthwise and, with a pair of scissors, shape the bottom half into an arc. Then cut a point and continue cutting straight to the top of the paper. Unfold the paper, place it on top of your fabric, and cut out four place mats.

2.   Cut the bias tape and glue it around the edges of your fabric. It's fine to piece your bias tape together — don't worry if it is not one seamless piece.

Sur la Table

We all daydream of a quaint dinner in the French countryside, don't we? Cover your table with this subtle, graceful tablecloth and you will instantly begin to hear the sounds of the Seine! Bonne chance!

TOOLS
scissors

needle

MATERIALS
burlap

muslin

dark-blue thread

1.   Cut or combine pieces of burlap to fit the size of your table.

2.   Depending on the size of your tablecloth, cut your muslin into 8-x-8-inch to 12-x-12-inch squares.

3.   Lay the muslin squares on top of the burlap in a bunched-up pile.

4.   With a needle and thread, perform a simple in-and-out stitch, attaching your muslin patches to the burlap, keeping the informal bunched-up pile intact.

I have yet to find a foolproof method to chop
or slice onions without tearing up . . . but
I can tell you one that makes you look so
silly that it takes your mind off your running
mascara. Put a match in between your teeth
and slice away!

Caramelized Onion Tart

SERVES 4–6

INGREDIENTS

¹/₂ stick butter

5 onions, thinly sliced

2 teaspoons fresh thyme,
roughly chopped

¹/₄ teaspoon grated nutmeg

1 package puff pastry dough

salt and pepper

1 cup grated Gruyère cheese

1. Preheat the oven to 350 degrees.

2. Melt the butter in a skillet. Add the onions and cook over medium heat, stirring periodically, until tender and lightly browned. Remove from heat.

3. Add the thyme and nutmeg, then season with salt and pepper. Set the onion mixture aside to cool.

4. Roll out the dough to form a rough rectangle.

5. Sprinkle the Gruyère onto the dough and top with onions. Fold the edges over to create a rim.

6. Bake until golden brown, about 20 minutes.

INGREDIENTS

1 pound frisée

4 eggs

2 tablespoons vinegar, for poaching

½ pound bacon, diced

2 tablespoons chopped shallots

3 tablespoons red wine vinegar

salt and pepper

1. Tear the frisée into bite-size pieces. Put into a large bowl.

2. Poach the eggs, following the directions in the note below.

3. Cook the bacon over medium heat, stirring occasionally until golden. Remove from pan. Add the shallots, stir, and cook for approximately 1 minute.

4. Add the red wine vinegar and boil for 5 seconds.

5. Pour the hot dressing over the frisée and toss with the bacon broken into bits.

6. Drain the eggs and serve on top of the salad. Season with salt and pepper.

BASIC 1-2-3 To poach eggs, boil water in a pot, add vinegar, and bring to a low simmer. Crack one egg into a small bowl. With a kitchen spoon, stir the water in a clockwise motion. Slide the egg out of the bowl and into the water. Poach for 3 minutes. With a slotted spoon, remove the poached egg and place in a bowl of cold water until ready to serve.

Frisée Salad
with Bacon and Poached Egg

Paul, the photographer of this book, took special care when shooting this salad. It's a longtime favorite of his because it reminds him of days spent in Paris watching his favorite soccer team.

SERVES 4–6

INGREDIENTS

4 tablespoons butter

4 skinless, boneless chicken breasts

salt and pepper

1/2 cup white wine

3/4 cup heavy cream

1 teaspoon Dijon mustard

2 tablespoons chopped parsley

1. Melt the butter in a large sauté pan, over medium heat.

2. Season the chicken on both sides with salt and pepper.

3. Turn the heat up to high, add the chicken, and sear on one side until golden brown, approximately 5 minutes. Repeat on the other side. Reduce heat to medium, and sauté until the chicken is cooked through. Remove from pan.

4. Add the white wine to the same pan to deglaze, scraping up any browned bits. Continue cooking over medium heat until the liquids have been reduced by about half.

5. Add the heavy cream and bring to a low boil. Turn down the heat and add the mustard and chopped parsley. Stir to combine.

6. Season with salt and pepper to taste. Pour the sauce over the chicken or add the chicken back to the pan to coat with sauce.

Dijon Chicken

I always tell people to start with eggs when they are first learning to cook . . . then move on to soups, next extra-simple recipes that have the appearance of being difficult so you will feel that you are getting somewhere. This is one of those recipes.

Mousse
au Chocolat

For chocolate lovers, this recipe will not disappoint!

SERVES 6

INGREDIENTS

2 cups dark chocolate

2 tablespoons butter

2 eggs

4 egg whites

5 tablespoons sugar

2 cups heavy cream

1. Put chocolate in a heatproof bowl over a saucepan of simmering water. Do not let the bottom of the bowl touch the water. Allow the chocolate to soften, then stir until melted.

2. Add the butter to the chocolate and stir until melted Remove the bowl from the saucepan and allow to cool for a few minutes.

3. Add the eggs and stir to combine.

4. Using a mixer, beat the egg whites, adding the sugar gradually, until soft peaks form. Whisk ⅓ of the egg whites into the chocolate mixture to loosen it, then fold in the remaining egg whites.

5. Whip the cream and fold it into the mousse mixture.

6. Pour the mousse into glasses, cover, and refrigerate for a few hours before serving.

KEEP IT SIMPLE You can melt the chocolate in a microwave oven. Heat it on high for 2 minutes and then stir.

Cinnamon Bread 9/25

Bran Muffin   9/25

Blueberry Muffin 9/25

As a youth, I had many bad habits and most of them involved the condition of my bedroom. My mother would say, "Pick your clothes up off the floor." I would proceed to toss them in my dirty-clothes hamper and, *presto chango,* one tidy room. This was hardly a method satisfying to my mother . . . *grounded!* "Make your bed before you leave for school," she would say, and I escaped without doing so, only to come home to my mom's unhappiness . . . *grounded!* "Fold your clean clothes." But isn't it much easier to just toss them in the drawers as is? Again, it was not what my mother had instructed . . . *grounded!*

Then there was my sister Lynn . . . a true Felix Unger. Forget that her bed was so well made you could bounce quarters off it or that nothing ever touched her bedroom floor but her feet, it was her closet that really made me green with envy: hanger after hanger of excellently selected and well-cared-for garments. Why did her clothes look so much better than mine? As much as I would try, I could never replicate her attention to organizational details; I truly lusted after her ways. When she wasn't looking I would sneak into her room and borrow whatever item struck my fancy. After carefully wearing the item, I would gingerly return the article, making *painstakingly* certain I had placed it in its exact place, folding it *precisely* the way I had found it. My caper never worked because that neat freak claimed I was such a walking mess that she could instantly see that I had invaded her area, pinpointing the exact item I had snatched. Yes, I was most certainly the Pigpen in my house.

Then as I grew up and accumulated responsibilities, I found that life as a slob no longer worked for me: it was extremely impractical. My lack of organization left me very inefficient. I was always late and disheveled and *not* on top of my game — I realized it was time to develop new habits. I had started a catering company, so my kitchen had to run like a well-oiled machine. Having a game plan was a necessity in order to get everything bought, cooked, and delivered. The more on top of things I was, the more successful, happy, and fulfilled I became.

If you too struggle with the world of order, or if you find your organized life has gotten away from you, then this chapter is for you. I say start with the kitchen, followed by your paperwork, and then find other piles to weed through. I think you will agree with my sister that being a neat freak is the best compliment someone can give you.

good clean fun

NEAT FREAK

IN THE KITCHEN

Have you ever heard people say, "I never get out of my kitchen"? Or "I spent the entire week slaving over the stove"? Or "All I ever seem to do is cook"? First, you must remember that the soul of any well-lived-in home is the kitchen, full of the great smells and the lure of that next yummy thing coming out of the oven. So it is *never* wrong to spend time keeping the fridge full and the stove cranking.

The crime is not finding a balance — that is, finding equal time for all things you and your family love. So I say, get organized! Dedicate one day of your precious weekend to preparing your weekly menu, filling your fridge with baking mixes that can be cooked at a moment's notice, and preparing your pantry with your most frequently used spice blends. I promise these organizational steps will make for a much happier and peaceful week . . . a week when you will find yourself saying, "Boy, we ate well and I didn't even slave over the stove!"

I like to get a jump on the week, and a great way to do that is by getting my menus organized. Start with a big cook-off on Mondays. By "big," I mean cook enough of one base ingredient for the rest of the week's recipes. Then all I have to do is dress up that base ingredient according to my recipes. The following ten recipes start with one big idea and proceed throughout the week to keep your tummies full. All recipes serve 4.

Whole Lemon Roasted Chicken

Will last, using the recipes that follow, throughout the week

INGREDIENTS

3 whole chickens, about 4 pounds each

salt and pepper

2 lemons, quartered

3 small onions, quartered

6 tablespoons butter, softened

1.   Preheat oven to 350 degrees. Clean cavities of chickens and season with salt and pepper.

2.   Loosely stuff lemon and onion quarters into the cavity of each chicken. Tie chicken legs together with twine.

3.   Place chickens in roasting pan. Rub butter over skin of each chicken, then season with salt and pepper.

4.   Roast chickens for about 1¼ hours, basting occasionally with pan juices.

TUESDAY:

BBQ Chicken Sandwich

INGREDIENTS

2 pounds leftover roast chicken

1 bottle BBQ sauce

4 buns, toasted

¹/₂ pound coleslaw

¹/₂ pound sliced cheddar cheese

1.   Shred chicken into large pieces.

2.   Heat BBQ sauce in a saucepan. Toss chicken with as much BBQ sauce as you like.

3.   Spoon BBQ chicken onto toasted bun. Top with coleslaw and cheddar cheese.

Chicken Lettuce Wraps with Peanut Sauce

INGREDIENTS

2 pounds leftover roast chicken

$^{1}/_{2}$ pound thin rice noodles or angel hair pasta

1–2 heads Boston lettuce, washed and dried

1 large cucumber, peeled, seeded, and julienned

2 large carrots, peeled and julienned

1 whole bell pepper, julienned

For Peanut Sauce

juice of 1 lime

3 tablespoons soy sauce

3 tablespoons peanut butter

4 teaspoons brown sugar

1 clove garlic, minced

4 tablespoons warm water

2 teaspoons grated ginger

1. Shred chicken into large pieces.

2. Prepare rice noodles or pasta according to directions on package.

3. In a small bowl, combine all ingredients for the peanut sauce.

4. For each wrap, top a lettuce leaf with noodles, chicken, and vegetables. Fold over and serve with peanut sauce on the side.

Hearty Chicken Corn Chowder

INGREDIENTS

2 pounds leftover roast chicken,
cut into small cubes

4 ounces cooked bacon, diced

1 large onion, chopped

4 cups (1 pound) corn kernels, frozen

2 large potatoes, diced

2 tablespoons thyme, fresh

$1/4$ cup flour

6 cups chicken stock/broth

1 can creamed corn

1 cup heavy cream

$1/4$ pound cheddar cheese, grated

1. In a large pot, cook bacon over medium-low heat, until crisp. Remove bacon and reserve fat in pan.

2. Add onions to bacon fat and sauté until softened. Add frozen corn kernels, potatoes, and thyme. Add flour and stir. Cook about 3 minutes.

3. Add stock/broth and creamed corn to pot. Bring to boil, then reduce heat and simmer about 30 minutes. Add cream and cheese and stir through. Cook until heated about 10 minutes.

Country Chicken Hash

INGREDIENTS

1 pound russet potatoes, peeled and cubed

3 tablespoons butter

2 pounds leftover roast chicken, diced

1 cup diced onion

1 whole bell pepper, diced

3 cloves minced garlic

1 cup diced Golden Delicious apple

1 teaspoon sage, dried

salt and pepper

3 tablespoons chicken stock

1 tablespoon Worcestershire sauce

2 tablespoons chopped fresh parsley

1. Boil or steam potatoes for 5–7 minutes. Drain and dry. (Potatoes will not be tender.)

2. In a large skillet, melt butter, add potatoes, and sauté until browned. Add chicken, onion, bell pepper, garlic, apple, and sage. Season with salt and pepper.

3. Stir in chicken stock and Worcestershire sauce and cook until heated through.

4. Add parsley and stir to combine.

Colorful Oven Roasted Vegetables

Will last, using the recipes that follow, throughout the week

INGREDIENTS

1 (10-ounce) package mushrooms

10 plum tomatoes, halved

1 eggplant, cut into large cubes

3 bunches asparagus

2 bunches carrots

1 butternut squash, cut into large cubes

6 bell peppers (red, yellow, green, orange), halved

4 zucchinis or yellow squashes, halved

2 bunches broccoli, cut into large pieces

3 red onions, quartered

olive oil

salt and pepper

1. Preheat oven to 375 degrees.

2. Sort vegetables according to how long they will take to roast. For example, place broccoli with asparagus in the same pan at same time. In another pan, or approximately five minutes later in the same pan, add zucchini or yellow squash, eggplant, tomatoes, mushrooms, and onions. And add butternut squash, peppers, and carrots last. This way, nothing will get overcooked.

3. Toss vegetables with olive oil, salt and pepper, and place them in pan.

4. Roast for 25-30 minutes.

Asparagus & Spinach Frittata

INGREDIENTS

olive oil

1 shallot, chopped

$1/2$ cup frozen spinach, thawed and drained

$1/2$ of the roasted asparagus, cut into 1-inch pieces

8 eggs

$1/4$ teaspoon nutmeg

salt and pepper

2 tablespoons water

1. Preheat oven to 425 degrees.

2. Heat oil in a large sauté pan. Sauté shallots until softened. Add spinach and asparagus.

3. Whisk eggs, nutmeg, salt, and pepper with water. Add egg mixture to pan and bake until eggs are almost set, about 5 minutes.

4. Place frittata under broiler until golden brown, about 2 minutes.

Fettuccine Primavera Tossed in a Raspberry Dressing

INGREDIENTS

1 pound fettuccine

2 of the roasted peppers, sliced into strips

$1/2$ of the roasted asparagus spears, cut into 2-inch pieces

$1/3$ of the roasted broccoli, cut into bite-size pieces

$1/4$ of the roasted mushrooms

$1/4$ of the roasted zucchini and squash

$1/2$ of the roasted onions

For Dressing

$1/4$ cup raspberry vinegar

2 teaspoons mustard

4 roasted tomatoes

salt and pepper

$1/2$–$3/4$ cup olive oil

1. Cook pasta according to instructions on package.

2. Make dressing: in a blender, combine vinegar, mustard, tomatoes, and salt and pepper. Add olive oil in a steady stream. Set aside.

3. While pasta is still hot, in a large bowl, toss it with heated vegetables and dressing.

THURSDAY:

Chunky Veggie & Sausage Pizzas

INGREDIENTS

1 package frozen pizza dough

$1/4$ of the roasted butternut squash

$1/2$ cup goat cheese

1 tablespoon chopped thyme

Prepare pizza dough according to instructions on package. Top with butternut squash, goat cheese, and thyme. Bake until dough is cooked and browned on edges.

INGREDIENTS

1 package frozen pizza dough

mozzarella cheese

$1/2$ of the roasted mushrooms

$1/2$ of the roasted onions

2 of the roasted bell peppers, cut into strips

2–3 links Italian sausage, cooked and broken into small pieces

Prepare pizza dough according to instructions on package. Top with mozzarella, mushrooms, onions, bell peppers, and sausage. Bake until dough is cooked and browned on edges.

FRIDAY:

Simple Stir-Fry with Scallions

INGREDIENTS

olive oil

1 tablespoon julienned ginger

2 cloves garlic, minced

$1/4$ pound snow peas

$1/3$ of the roasted broccoli, cut into bite-size pieces

$1/2$ of the roasted peppers, cut into large dice

$1/4$ of the zucchini/squash cut into large dice

$1/2$ of the carrots, sliced into rounds

$1/2$ of the roasted eggplant

2 green onions, thinly sliced

For sauce

4 tablespoons soy sauce

1 teaspoon sesame oil

1 teaspoon cornstarch

2 tablespoons hoisin sauce

pinch of sugar

$1/4$ cup water

1. In a bowl, combine all sauce ingredients. Mix until the cornstarch is dissolved. Set aside.

2. Add oil to a hot wok or skillet and sauté ginger and garlic. Add sauce and bring to boil, cooking until thickened. Add vegetables and heat through. Remove from heat.

3. Sprinkle with green onion on top. Serve with rice.

Where do I begin with this recipe? So many memories . . .
so many stories . . . so many good smells. It was the thing
I most loved waking up to; it was the thing I delivered to
the new neighbors. It's rumored to be my aunt Ruth's
recipe, but many others have tried to claim it as their own.
It's the recipe I'm sure is the most destined to become
your new family classic.

Cinnamon Bread

MAKES 2–4 LOAVES
(DEPENDING ON SIZE)

INGREDIENTS

2 cups sugar

1 cup shortening

4 eggs

2 teaspoons vanilla extract

4 cups flour

2 teaspoons baking soda

2 teaspoons baking powder

1 teaspoon salt

2 cups buttermilk

For Cinnamon Mixture

2 teaspoons cinnamon
(more, if you like)

½ cup sugar

1. Preheat oven to 350 degrees.

2. Cream sugar and shortening together. Beat in eggs and vanilla. Set aside.

3. In a bowl, combine flour, baking soda, baking powder, and salt.

4. Alternately add buttermilk and flour mixture to the egg mixture, beginning and ending with the buttermilk.

5. For cinnamon mixture: in a bowl, mix cinnamon into sugar to combine. Set aside.

6. Pour half the batter into 2 large greased loaf pans or 4 smaller ones. Sprinkle with half of the cinnamon mixture. Layer the other half of the batter on top and sprinkle with other half of cinnamon mixture.

7. Using a knife, cut through the batter to swirl in the cinnamon mixture.

8. Bake for 45 minutes to 1 hour, depending on the size of your loaf pans, or until a knife comes out clean.

YES YOU CAN Prepare the batter and refrigerate it for up to 10 days.

Make-Ahead Spice Mixes

It's just so much easier to give a little zest and zip to your cuisine if your spices are premixed. Nothin' like having the essence of pie, the lustiness of Italy, and the heat of chili available with the simple shake of a wrist!

Poultry Spice Mix

INGREDIENTS

1 tablespoon tarragon, dried

2 tablespoons parsley, dried

2 tablespoons sage, dried

2 tablespoons marjoram, dried

1 tablespoon garlic salt

1 tablespoon black pepper, ground

1 tablespoon lemon zest

Combine all ingredients. Store in cool, dark place.

Chili Spice Mix

INGREDIENTS

3 tablespoons chili powder

2 tablespoons paprika

1 tablespoon cumin powder

1 tablespoon oregano, dried

2 tablespoons garlic salt

1 tablespoon black pepper, ground

Combine all ingredients. Store in cool, dark place.

Pie Spice Mix

INGREDIENTS

2 tablespoons cinnamon

1 tablespoon ginger

1 teaspoon cloves

1 teaspoon nutmeg

1 teaspoon allspice

Combine all ingredients. Store in cool, dark place.

MAKE IT CHIC Store your spice mixes in restaurant-style sugar shakers. Cut out a fabric square, bigger than the shaker opening, and then cut a circle within the square for the spices to shake out of. Print the name of the spice with a permanent marker on the fabric square.

IN THE BOARDROOM

"In the boardroom we . . ." I just like the sound of that. I always feel only the most efficient and productive people start sentences using those words. I would like to put an end to that. I view all of the next organizational projects as if someone were assembling a boardroom of sorts — the tools of the trade, if you will. If you're a person who needs to improve her bottom line when it comes to thank-you notes, gift wrapping, cleaning, or memory note-pads . . . these projects will help you get organized. Have some fun this weekend getting *your* boardroom together.

That's a Wrap!

Wrapping paper, ribbons, tape, scissors — where are they when you need them? Here's the solution: transform a simple, inexpensive trunk into a place for gift wrapping and gift wrapping *alone*. Turn the top into a cushioned seat so you can take a load off after wrapping all the gifts!

TOOLS	MATERIALS
tape measure	trunk
scissors	fabric
staple gun	batting
hot-glue gun	ribbon
iron	Stitch Witchery
	curtain tension rod

TOP OF TRUNK

1. Measure the top of your trunk and cut a piece of fabric 8 inches wider on all four sides.

2. Cut a piece of batting to the size of the top of your trunk and stack it about 4–5 inches thick. Lay the batting down on top of your trunk, center the fabric over the top, and wrap the fabric neatly around the lid, stapling to the underside of the lid.

3. Using hot glue, cover your staples with decorative ribbon.

INSIDE POCKETS

4. Cut three strips of fabric of equal width, big enough to fully cover the empty space on the inside lid of your trunk.

5. Fold the top and sides of each strip of the fabric to make a hem and iron with Stitch Witchery.

6. Turn the top strip into a pocket by hot-gluing it to the inside lid around the two sides and bottom edges. Repeat for the next two strips, overlapping them by $1/4$ inch as you go.

BRIGHT IDEA To hold your ribbons, suspend a thin curtain tension rod in the back section of your trunk.

MAKE IT CHIC Either buy an inexpensive trunk or refurbish one that you already have.

Notes at a Glance

Always searching for a place to jot down a phone number? Or a shopping list? Or a reminder? With this nifty wall pad, your paper searching troubles are over!

TOOLS

hot-glue gun

MATERIALS

Post-its (multiple sizes)

24 x 24-inch wood board

1. Arrange Post-it pads on wood board, some with edges touching and some with spaces in between.

2. Apply two dots of hot glue to the top corners of the pad and hold in place until it sticks onto the wood board.

DID YOU KNOW? We leaned this up against our wall, but if you want to hang it, just get yourself a screwdriver and a picture-hanging kit.

YOU CAN'T GO WRONG When your pad runs out, just hot-glue another of the same size on top.

Thank You, Thank You!

We always have good intentions when needing to write thank-you notes. We have personal stationery printed and our stamps at the ready, but getting the materials organized to send them is an eternal quandary. Here's an idea: create a foolproof way to get your thank-you notes out in time and give gratitude its own station in your home. I promise, your loved one will feel thoroughly and utterly appreciated.

TOOLS

pinking shears

hole punch

MATERIALS

fabric

Stitch Witchery, 3/4 inch wide

3 file folders

leather cord

1. Using your pinking shears, cut a 15-by-34-inch piece of fabric for your backing. For the pockets, cut 3 13 1/4- by-9 1/2-inch pieces of the same fabric.

2. Lay flat your piece of backing and evenly space your three pockets on top. Attach your pockets on both short sides and one long side using Stitch Witchery.

3. Label your 3 file folders and slip them into your pockets.

4. Punch three holes, evenly spaced, along one short side of the fabric and knot a piece of 3-foot leather cord through each hole.

5. Fold up your pockets and wrap the cord around haphazardly.

A-Bucket-a-Room

Housekeeping is a wishy-washy habit — sometimes you're in the mood to get down to the nitty-gritty, but other times getting it done seems like the grandest of chores. You can make your life *much* easier by dividing up your cleaning supplies as they pertain to each room. With this system, one can never say, "But I couldn't find the floor cleaner!"

TOOLS

scissors

scallop shears

hole punch

wire cutters

MATERIALS

Clip art images or drawings of each room

step flashing (metal squares)

adhesive laminating sheets

wire

mini clipboards

buckets

BUCKET LABELS

1. Cut your image to approximately 4 inches wide, leaving a bit of space around the borders.

2. Using the scallop shears, cut your step flashing to 5-by-5-inch squares.

3. Cut a piece of your laminating material about ¼ inch wider on each side than your clip art printout. Peel off the backing of the laminate sheet and adhere the art to the center of a metal square.

4. Using your punch, punch a hole at the top center of the square, about ¼ inch down from the top edge. Thread your wire through and attach to the handle of your bucket.

CLIPBOARD LABELS AND CHARTS

5. Using laminating sheets, adhere copies of the same images to the back of your mini clipboard. Store the clipboards in the buckets.

6. Create a cleaning log chart that will tell you when the rooms were last cleaned and by whom.

Wipe Away Your Washing Woes!

We spend so much time dreading the process of housework, but if you were able to visit a cool cleaning center in your laundry room, perhaps you would be more inspired to get the job done! Cleaning supplies should have an attractive place to live, too.

TOOLS

drill

paintbrush

painter's tape

wire cutters

staple gun

MATERIALS

shelf brackets

12-by-48-inch plywood board (or ready-made particle board shelf)

paint

garden border wire

screw hooks

1. Drill brackets into wall.

2. Paint the shelf the color of your choice.

3. Using your painter's tape, outline a rectangle the width of your shelf and 12 inches high. Fill in your rectangle with paint, thus creating a backsplash.

4. Using wire cutters, clip garden border wire at the bottom, where the arches begin, and attach it to the front edge of the shelf with a staple gun.

5. Screw hooks into the bottom of shelf, one per bucket.

HERE TO STAY Use anchors because this shelf is going to have a great deal of weight on it!

Current Events Cubbies

Magazines can get unruly — you swear you're going to read them, but they just pile up around you uncontrollably. This magazine mayhem can be managed by these simple, out-of-the-way wall-mounted racks.

TOOLS

scissors

hot-glue gun

hammer

MATERIALS

11-by-14-inch shadow box

$\frac{1}{4}$-inch dowel

decorative label letters

nails

double-stick mounting squares

1. Remove the glass and the back of the frame from the shadow box.

2. Using your scissors, cut the dowel to the inside width of the opening of the frame and hot-glue it in place about a third of the way up, on the inside of the frame.

3. Hot-glue label letters onto the outside edge of the frame.

4. Hammer two nails into the wall, the width of the inside dimensions of your frame apart. You want your frame to fit snuggly over these nails so as not to fall off with the weight of your magazines. Place mounting squares on the bottom corners.

Doodle Desk

We should all encourage our kids' imaginations, but with that comes a mess of markers, crayons, paints, glue, and glitter. Here's a solution that not only keeps your kids' art stations neat and tidy but also transforms your munchkins into modern masters!

TOOLS

scissors

hammer

small nails

MATERIALS

self-adhesive Velcro

picture frame (glass and back removed)

child's table

newsprint pad

4 canvas paintbrush holders

1.   Adhere Velcro along the sides of the back of the frame and to the surface of the table.

2.   Insert pad into frame and then Velcro the frame to the table.

3.   Hammer your small nails through the paintbrush holders into each side of the table. Fill the pockets with art supplies.

YOU CAN'T GO WRONG Any size desk will work — just make sure you choose a frame that's a bit smaller than the tabletop, and a pad that fits inside the frame.

Petoskey, Michigan, is a small town on the shores of Lake Michigan— a town unlike any other town in the whole United States of America. It is *magic*. Yes, that's right. If they asked me to do an infomercial for my hometown of Petoskey, I would. It is simply a *jewel*. But not because of its sophistication, its vicinity to any large metropolis, its large arts community, or its stellar school system. No, no, no. Petoskey is a jewel because of its reverence for the great outdoors. I don't know who the town benefactors were before I grew up there, but I do know that I am grateful for their wisdom. You see, as a child in this majestic northern community, I had so many ways to enjoy Mother Nature. Where do I begin? There was the deer park, the state park, Magnus Park, and on and on and on.

In the depths of the winter, the place to be was the Winter Sports Park. And what a park it was! It had everything you could want in a winter wonderland: a rope tow for the skier, a huge rink complete with a rustic warming hut that piped out the greatest music du jour, many sledding hills that featured an apparatus unique to Petoskey, the Bump Jumper. This is a single-rider, single-ski seat sure to thrill even the most experienced of tobogganers.

Then the ice would thaw, and it was off to another popular spot: the Boardwalk. As the name implies, this is a boarded trail through the woods of the Upper Peninsula. My mother would pack a picnic, pile us in the car, and awalking we would go. She always had a guide-book in hand, informing us of the plant life around us. We would trail close behind her, picking up nature's treasures that had fallen to the ground for further study at home. Yes, if I could move back I would, but my husband says not until palm trees grow there.

This chapter is dedicated to my hometown in hopes that it will encourage everyone to take a weekend and find ways to enjoy nature's great outdoors.

GREAT *forest inspirations*
OUTDOORS

NATURE TRAILS

Have you ever noticed that food tastes better when eaten outside — whether a picnic at the beach, a snack after a walk in the woods, or even a meal cooked over a bonfire? If the answer to the above question is yes, then this weekend's section is for you. We have developed some simple, quick, and delicious ways to bring the flavors of the dining table to the natural outdoor trails. Whether you are going for a quick walk or making a day and an evening of it, the following recipes will help make your outing unforgettable.

Dig In!

We all love a picnic, but serving food outdoors and having the utensils that you need can sometimes be a drag. You can streamline the whole process by making these simple yet fun envelopes to hold your plastic eating utensils.

TOOLS
salad plate
pencil
scissors
hole punch

MATERIALS
decorative paper
plastic tableware
green raffia

1. Trace the outline of a salad plate on the back side of the paper and cut it out.

2. Fold the circle a quarter of the way up, creating a pocket.

3. Fold in the left and right sides so that they overlap by ½ inch in the center.

4. To make slots, lay your plastic ware on top of the pouch. Mark 2 dots in between each utensil, vertically, about 1 inch apart. Using the hole punch, punch holes in these spots.

5. Thread 2 pieces of raffia vertically through each set of holes and tie in a knot.

6. Insert plastic ware.

SERVES 4–6

INGREDIENTS

1½ pounds flank steak

1 zucchini, cut into strips lengthwise

5 ounces (about 9) button mushrooms, sliced

olive oil

salt and pepper

1 jar roasted red peppers, cut into strips

string

2 tablespoons chopped parsley

1 tablespoon chopped thyme

1. Trim any excess fat off the beef. Carefully butterfly the steak so it opens up like a book.

2. Coat zucchini strips and mushroom slices with a little oil and salt and pepper, and cook in a grill pan for a couple of minutes on each side.

3. With steak opened up, layer zucchini, mushrooms, and red pepper strips inside. Close up the steak and secure it with kitchen string.

4. Rub steak with olive oil and sprinkle with chopped parsley, thyme, salt, and pepper.

5. Grill steak on each side for about 5–7 minutes or until done to your liking. Allow it to rest for 10 minutes before slicing.

Stuffed Flank Steak

This is a great menu for a cookout whether it's a sunny summer afternoon, a crisp fall evening, or a winter sledding party. Pack up your baskets, fill up your thermos, and don't forget the matches!

Thyme for Corn!

SERVES 6

INGREDIENTS

6 ears corn, husks left on

6 tablespoons butter, cut into pats

thyme sprigs

1. Soak corn in a pot of water for 1 hour.

2. Gently peel back the corn husks, being careful not to detach them, and remove the silk.

3. Pull the husks back up around the corn. Tuck a few pats of butter and a couple of sprigs of thyme into the husks. Make sure the husks completely cover the corn.

4. Grill corn for about 15 minutes, turning frequently.

Parchment Packet
Potatoes

SERVES 6–8

INGREDIENTS

thyme sprigs

1 teaspoon paprika

1 teaspoon minced garlic

1 teaspoon each salt and pepper

2 pounds Yukon gold potatoes, cut into quarters

1 small sweet onion, sliced

olive oil

parchment paper

aluminum foil

1. In a large bowl, combine herbs and seasonings with potatoes and onion. Drizzle with olive oil and toss to coat.

2. Rip off a piece of parchment paper large enough to make an envelope for the potatoes. Place the potatoes in the middle of the paper and fold it over. Wrap the entire parchment envelope in foil.

3. Grill the packets for 30–35 minutes, or until the potatoes are tender.

Designer Breadsticks

Having a hard time getting your family off the couch? Here's a great way to start them moving. Entice the troops into the outdoors by packing up some simple snacks and designer drinks. What better way to get your couch potatoes walking in the woods than with the warm smell of chocolate, the bright punch of berries, the warm scent of flavored breadsticks?

SERVES 4–6

INGREDIENTS

1 package breadstick dough

olive oil

toppings (see below)

1. Preheat oven according to directions on breadstick package.

2. Separate dough into strips and place on a baking sheet.

3. Add toppings as you please and twist dough around the fillings. (Don't worry if some fall out.)

4. Bake as directed.

Breadstick Toppings

PARMESAN-PROSCIUTTO: Spread dough with Dijon-style mustard. Layer with thinly sliced prosciutto and grated Parmesan cheese.

PESTO: Slather dough with pesto sauce. Top with pine nuts.

HERB BLEND: Brush dough with olive oil. Top with chopped thyme and parsley. Sprinkle with salt.

TRAIL MIX: Coat dough with honey and sprinkle with cinnamon. Press raisin-nut trail mix into dough. Brush top with melted butter.

CHEESE: Brush dough with Italian salad dressing. Sprinkle with fresh Parmesan.

OLIVE-ROSEMARY: Press chopped pitted olives into dough. Twist to enclose olives. Drizzle top with olive oil and top with chopped fresh rosemary.

CHEDDAR-SAGE: Brush dough with olive oil. Sprinkle with shredded cheddar cheese, chopped sage, and paprika.

Irresistible
Pretzels

MAKES 25 STICKS

INGREDIENTS

2 cups pecans

1 cup white chocolate chips

1 cup butterscotch chips

1 cup chocolate chips

1 cup brown sugar, packed

$1/4$ cup butter

2 cups whipping cream

$1/2$ teaspoon vanilla extract

25 pretzel rods

1. In a food processor, coarsely chop pecans and chips. Put into a large bowl and set aside.

2. In a small saucepan, combine brown sugar, butter, and whipping cream. Bring to a boil over medium heat and simmer, stirring constantly, for about 15 minutes.

3. Remove from heat and stir in vanilla. Cool until slightly thickened, about 15–20 minutes.

4. Dip each pretzel into caramel mixture, covering about $1/3$ of the pretzel. Let caramel drip off slightly.

5. Spoon or roll the chopped-nut-and-chip mixture onto the caramel pretzel. Let stand on wax paper or foil until caramel has set.

A Twist on S'mores

SERVES 4 OF EACH KIND (FOR EACH VARIATION)

White Chocolate & Berry Jam S'mores

INGREDIENTS

4 marshmallows

1 8-ounce bar white chocolate

8 gingersnap cookies

4 tablespoons berry jam, any kind

1. Toast marshmallows. Place a piece of white chocolate and a marshmallow on one of the gingersnaps.

2. Spoon jam over marshmallows and sandwich with gingersnap.

Peanut Butter Cup S'mores

INGREDIENTS

4 marshmallows

4 peanut butter cups

8 graham crackers

Toast marshmallows. Sandwich peanut butter cups and marshmallows between your crackers.

Chocolate Mint S'mores

INGREDIENTS

4 marshmallows

4 chocolate mints

8 chocolate wafer cookies

Toast marshmallows. Sandwich chocolate mint candy and marshmallows between your crackers.

Dreamy Chocolate Toffee

SERVES 4–6

INGREDIENTS

$\frac{1}{2}$ cup finely chopped pecans

$\frac{1}{2}$ cup butter

$\frac{3}{4}$ cup brown sugar

$\frac{1}{2}$ cup semisweet chocolate chips

$\frac{1}{4}$ cup flaked coconut

1 teaspoon cinnamon

Note: You'll need a candy thermometer for this recipe.

1.   Sprinkle the pecans over the bottom of a buttered 8-by-8-by-2-inch baking pan.

2.   In a small saucepan, combine the butter and brown sugar. Cook over medium heat, stirring constantly, until the mixture comes to a boil. Continue cooking until it registers 295 degrees on a candy thermometer.

3.   Remove the butter-and-sugar mixture from the heat and immediately pour it over the pecans, spreading it out evenly. Sprinkle with the chocolate chips, coconut, and cinnamon and let set for 5 minutes. When the chips have melted, spread them and the coconut and cinnamon evenly over the top.

4.   When the toffee has set, break it into bite-size pieces.

TOFFEE & PEPPERMINT
Hot Chocolate

SERVES 4

INGREDIENTS

4 cups milk

$\frac{1}{2}$ cup water

$\frac{1}{2}$ cup sugar

8 ounces bittersweet or semisweet chocolate, coarsely chopped

1 bar toffee candy and peppermint candies, crushed

1.   In saucepan, combine milk, water, and sugar. Stir over medium heat until mixture comes to a boil. Remove from heat.

2.   Stir in chocolate. Whisk until chocolate is melted and mixture is frothy. Pour into thermos.

3.   To serve, pour hot chocolate into cup and top with crushed candy.

Scarlet Punch

SERVES 8

INGREDIENTS

1 package (10 ounces) frozen strawberries

1 can jellied cranberry sauce

6 cups ginger ale or club soda

1.   In a blender, puree strawberries and cranberry sauce.

2.   Stir in ginger ale or club soda.

3.   Fill empty water bottles with punch.

NATURAL DESIGNS

Mother Nature has always been my greatest influence when it comes to style. In my homes I try to mirror her casual elegance, disciplined use of color, earthy manner, and element of surprise. Sometimes I find this more of a challenge than others, for she is a tough role model. So, I often resort to simple theft. This can be anything from literally taking an element from the outdoors and incorporating it into my design or simply re-creating one of her treasures. I hope the following projects encourage you to take a weekend, bring the outdoors in, and enjoy indulging in the inspirations borrowed from my mentor.

Sew Natural

In the winter, when the leaves have fallen from the trees, we long for the days of a green, leafy spring. You can preserve the beautiful delicacy of nature with this new spin on the framed, pressed leaf . . . and it's *sew* easy to do!

TOOLS
heavy books

thick needle
with large eye

scissors

MATERIALS
freshly picked leaves
or ferns

thick white art paper

string

green paper

ready-made frame

1.   Press your leaves between heavy books overnight.

2.   Place your leaves on the paper and use the needle to trace around and all the way to the top of the leaf stem by punching holes into your paper about every ¼ inch. Trace around the leafy part by punching holes about every 2 inches.

3.   Starting either at the top or at the bottom, sew the leaf to the paper using the holes you've punched and the needle and string. Tie knots at the beginning and end to serve as stoppers.

4.   Attach the white paper to the green paper by sewing a little "x" in each corner.

5.   Place the entire piece in the frame.

HERE TO STAY Consider using artificial leaves if you want the piece to stay green.

YOU CAN'T GO WRONG We used a simple in-and-out stitch, but feel free to be creative. You can vary your stitching to your preference: space your stitches out farther or closer together, as you prefer.

Luminous
Layers

As you stroll through the woods on your nature walk, look up, look down, look left and right. Take it all in: the trees, the flora, the branches, and the vines. You notice the sun shining through the leaves and wonder how you can package that beauty and live with it in your home.

TOOLS
scissors

MATERIALS
8 11 x 14-inch sheets of ⅛-inch-thick Plexiglas

7 leaves

leather cord

1.   Lay one piece of Plexiglas flat on the table, and place a leaf in the center. Repeat by laying a second piece of Plexiglas on top of the first and adding another leaf. Continue until you have used all 8 pieces of Plexiglas.

2.   Move the stack of Plexiglas to the edge of the table, with about 2 inches hanging off the edge. Cut a length of leather cord, wrap it tightly around the stack of Plexiglas several times, and tie a knot. Do the same for the other edge of the frame.

MAKE IT CHIC Keep it simple by using a single leaf per layer, varying the placement slightly so the leaves will overlap as you look through the Plexiglas.

tape measure

hammer

paper towel

twig or sprig with
an interesting shape

large photocopy

glue

1 long stick

2 6-inch sticks, each with
a Y-shaped hook or arm
that can act as a hook

nails

1. Take your sprig or twig to a copy store and enlarge it to approximately 60 inches high. Make sure to leave about 18 inches of extra paper at the top and bottom.

2. Back at home, roll up the extra paper at the top and bottom of the photocopy and apply a line of glue to both rolls to secure them.

3. Insert the long stick through the top roll, making sure it is long enough to leave about 5 inches sticking out on either side of the scroll.

4. Measure the width of your scroll, add 4 inches, and nail your "hook" sticks to the wall using this measurement.

5. Hang your scroll on the hooks.

DID YOU KNOW? Most large copy stores have a blueprint-copying machine, which we used for this project.

RULE OF THUMB To keep your scrolls looking round, you may want to stuff them with newspaper.

MAKE IT CHIC With a lighter, you can burn the edges of the paper to give it an antique look. Make sure to keep a damp paper towel close by to blot out the flame.

Larger than Life

Create natural drama in your home by turning a twig into a tree or a sprig into a larger-than-life leaf. All you need is a piece of the great outdoors and a copy machine, and you can create a beautiful, unique piece of art that will dress a wall from top to bottom.

TOOLS

tape measure

scissors

sponges

glue

hammer

MATERIALS

paper tree wrap

3 shades of green paint

googly eyes

paint markers

brown marker

artificial leaves

copper brads

1. Measure the length of the wall that you would like to decorate. Cut a piece of tree wrap to that length.

2. Cut circles and ovals of various sizes out of household sponges.

3. Dip a sponge into some paint and press onto the tree wrap. Continue stamping to make the full length of the bug. Repeat as many times as you have space for.

4. Glue googly eyes to the head of each bug.

5. With a brown marker, draw simple little lines for the bug's legs and antennae.

6. Glue artificial leaves to the back side and front edges of the border.

7. Attach border to the wall using a hammer and copper brads spaced every 12 inches.

Ants Marching

Bring creepy crawlers into your kids' decor
without bringing the real things into your home!

Orange You Hungry?

Add a splash of bold color to your backyard while serving up a snack to the sparrows and cardinals that live in your trees.

TOOLS

knife

spoon

1 long nail

scissors

MATERIALS

1 orange

sticks (8–10")

twine

small wooden beads

glue

birdseed

1. With the knife, cut off top of the orange, about ½ inch down, and scoop out the fruit with the spoon.

2. Use the nail to punch 4 holes through the orange rind, 2 pairs directly across from each other. Push sticks through the holes for the birds to sit on. (The sticks will go through the orange rind parallel.)

3. Cut 4 lengths of twine. Knot a length of twine around each stick where the stick meets the orange. Gather the 4 pieces of twine and knot them at the top. This will be the hanger for your bird feeder.

4. Cut 4 more lengths of twine, at varying lengths. Knot them together to create a tassel. Decorate it by sliding small, wooden beads onto the twine and securing them with dabs of glue.

5. Use the nail to punch a hole in the bottom of the orange. Push the knot up through the hole in the orange so that the tassel hangs down.

6. Pour birdseed into orange.

The Never-Ending Tree

Truly bring the outside in by re-creating a grapevine tree within the walls of your own home. The brilliant fact about this tree is that it will never need water, nor will it ever lose its leaves!

TOOLS

pencil

scissors

small nail

wire cutters

pliers

hammer

MATERIALS

a tree leaf with a simple but interesting shape

copper foil (roofing copper)

copper wire

grapevine wreath

copper brads

LEAVES:

1. Using the simple leaf that you found, trace the leaf shape onto the copper foil. Cut out the copper leaf using regular scissors.

2. With a small nail, punch a small hole about a ½ inch up from the bottom of the copper leaf.

3. Cut a piece of copper wire about 4 inches long. Thread the wire through the hole in the leaf.

4. With pliers, twist the wire around itself so it will stay in place.

5. Repeat steps 1–4 for the desired number of leaves.

TREE/VINE:

1. Unwrap the grapevine wreath by cutting the long piece of vine that holds it together. The pieces of the vine will then pull apart easily. Next cut or break into pieces varying in lengths from 5 to 9 feet.

2. Hold up your pieces to get a sense of where your tree will begin and end. When satisfied, attach the pieces to the wall by tacking two copper brads on either side of the grapevine, hence sandwiching it in place. Repeat this step along the entire length of the grapevine, hammering brads approximately every 2–5 feet.

3. Twist your copper leaf stems onto the vine.

YES, YOU CAN You can customize this project by installing the vine on a ceiling, along the top of a wall, up a post, or around a door.

Everybody's got them. They are as regular as ten fingers and ten toes, as American as apple pie, as common as the common cold. They happen every year, come rain or shine, sleet or snow. What are they, you ask? They are the HOLIDAYS. The time of year when seasons change, when the music gets jolly, when families become a lot more familiar and your home has the opportunity to sparkle and shine. I say it is worth every effort, every recipe, every ornament, and every well-sung song. I would not give up any of the following memories. From the matching green-and-white outfits delivered by my Uncle Moses on Christmas Eve, to my Grandmother Gladys and her Thanksgiving dresses. And I could never forget my Uncle Meredith's continually surprising gifts.

Yes, holidays exist to help us express affection toward those we love. I cannot wait until my daughter is old enough to enjoy the good things I plan to do to make her holiday memories complete. I can only hope I can make my mother proud, since she was the master at making the holidays seem special for us all. I often joke that I do for a living what my mother did for free. Like my mother, I will first decorate the door, followed by the tree, and then turn my attention to the meal, and oh yes, I can't forget the activity table complete with refreshments and crafts that will allow my daughter to participate in the festive holiday preparations. Everybody's got them and everybody should keep on doing them. Keep the holidays alive by taking a weekend and re-creating some of the following projects. Add a few of your own so that you and those you love can bask in the glow of a well-spent holiday.

all that sparkles & shines

HOLIDAY

DECK THE HALLS

I don't think there is anything more fun than setting a holiday mood — I know it helps me get in the spirit of the season. I realize the holidays are the time to give to those you love, but the truth is, as happy as my decked-out house makes my friends and family, it makes me even happier. As I decorate the corners of my home, I discover things about the architecture that I never noticed or appreciated. As I hang my seasonal trims, I smell scents that take me back to many happy times. So no matter what holiday you are preparing for, tackle the following projects and enjoy. If it is Thanksgiving, instead of a pine wreath try a straw version with pheasants. If it is New Year's Eve, stuff your bottles with New Year's resolutions and hide them to open the next year. If it is Easter, hang Easter eggs from a grapevine draped across your mantel. Pick your holiday, make the projects your own, and turn your holiday stress into true holiday spirit!

Adorn a Door

What is one of the first things many of us do around Christmastime? We hang a wreath on our front door, welcoming not only our guests and loved ones, but also the holidays into our home. This year, adorn your door with a wreath that combines nature's greenery and timber with a touch of sparkle that never fails to make the special. (See photo on page 168.)

TOOLS
wire cutters

MATERIALS
green pine wreath

grapevine wreath (approximately the size of the opening of the pine wreath)

silver spray glitter

floral wire

various kinds of ribbon

white feathers

white artificial birds

clear glass ornament balls

1. Take your grapevine wreath outside and spray it with silver spray glitter.

2. Center the grapevine wreath on top of the pine wreath and wrap floral wire through vine wreath and around the pine wreath.

3. Take your array of ribbons and wrap them around both wreaths, creating a striped effect.

4. Embellish with white feathers, artificial birds, and glass ornament balls.

Hang Your Hopes

The holiday season is about family and friends giving and receiving . . . wishes and dreams. When the holiday season is upon you, have everyone — adults and kids alike — write a message on a piece of paper. Slip these messages into a glass bottle or bird ornaments and the hopes and prayers of your loved ones will have a special home on your Christmas tree this year.

TOOLS	MATERIALS
spoon	glass message bottles
pen	double-sided tape
scissors	glitter
utility knife	strips of paper
	twine
	artificial birds
	wire

BOTTLES

1. Wrap the body of each glass bottle with 3 parallel strips of double-stick tape.

2. With a spoon, scoop and sprinkle glitter onto the tape.

3. Write special wishes on pieces of paper, roll them up, tie with twine, and slide each inside a bottle.

4. Tie a length of twine around the neck of each of the message bottles and hang them on your tree.

BIRDS

1. With a utility knife, cut a small slit in the beak of each bird.

2. Write special wishes on pieces of paper and slide them into the birds' beaks.

3. Use wire if necessary to attach birds to your tree.

3-2-1 Holiday!

The last week before the big holiday can be so much more stressful than fun. It seems no matter how much I swear that I am going to get everything done far in advance so I can enjoy the season, it never seems to happen. . . . so I have found a solution: reinvent the Advent calendar so that it focuses on those last seven pressure-filled days. Then fill it up with something that will brighten you or your loved ones' days . . . perhaps one of your favorite sayings, a yummy piece of candy, a sprig of your favorite herb — anything that will allow you to stop and take stock in the joy that is supposed to fill the days that lead up to the holiday. The great thing about our Advent calendar is we designed it in such a way that after you enjoy your reprieve it will hang anywhere and add a spot of beauty to your holiday decor, and it can be used year after year.

TOOLS

scissors

utility knife

nail scissors

hole punch

MATERIALS

elf images (you can print them from the Web or copy from coloring books)

craft glue

black velvet paper

small gift boxes

ribbon

small metal numbers, to denote dates

paper clips

1. To make an Advent box, begin by cutting a square around an elf image and dabbing a dot of glue on each corner. Attach the square onto the black velvet paper.

2. Using your utility knife or nail scissors, carefully cut out the elf's silhouette. (Depending on how many elf images you are using as patterns and how many silhouettes you need in all, you may need to make multiple silhouettes of each image.) With craft glue, glue the elf silhouette into the bottom (not the lid) of a box. Repeat for as many boxes as you want.

3. To hang each box, use the hole punch to punch 2 holes in the center of the top side of the bottom of the box and thread a ribbon through. Then tie a knot to create a loop.

4. Punch 2 holes in the center of the lid, thread the same ribbon through, and then tie into a bow with the metal number hanging down.

5. Place whatever object tickles your holiday fancy.

THE NIGHT BEFORE CHRISTMAS

When I was growing up, the absolute best thing about the holidays was our annual Christmas Eve party. Great food, good people, and my favorite part, the pageant. I never had a better run than when I got to be the little drummer boy in *The Little Drummer Boy*. You see, in previous plays I always played farm animals while my older sisters starred in roles such as Mary and the child in the Christmas pageant. I was left to toil away as the mouse in *Santa Mouse*, the donkey in the manger scene . . . you get the picture. But I had equally as much fun preparing the scenery, creating the curtain, and assembling the program. Now that I am much too old to stand up and be one of the wise men in front of my holiday guests, I focus on the fun that can be had creating the backdrop for a fantastic meal. Get out your glitter and your shine and adapt the following projects to fit your holiday. Then as the second act, direct your own holiday culinary performance.

A Dove's **Nest**

This year's theme of feathers and birds will appeal to that whimsical side of the holiday season, where everything you see is adorned with a bit of sparkle and shine. Combining the natural and whimsical will make this a holiday for all to remember! (See photo on page 174.)

MATERIALS

tall glass bowl vases

Spanish moss

green moss

feathers

tinsel

1. Fill the inside of each bowl vase with Spanish moss.

2. Add a layer of green moss on top.

3. Scatter feathers and tinsel sparsely in and around the moss to add sparkle and texture.

A holiday is not a holiday unless somebody does a lot of cooking. And for those who need cooking made easy, the following recipes comprise a great menu that will put anyone in a festive mood.

Rib Roast with Horseradish Sauce

Beet and Apple Salad

Green Bean Bundles

Mashed Root Vegetables

Shaved Fennel, Arugula, and Tangerine Salad

Delectable Pumpkin Cheesecake with a Chocolate Crust

Autumn Punch

ALL DISHES SERVE 6–8

Rib Roast WITH HORSERADISH SAUCE

Rib Roast

INGREDIENTS

1 6–8 pound rib roast

Salt and pepper

1. Preheat oven to 450 degrees.

2. Generously rub roast with salt and pepper.

3. Lay meat in a roasting pan, ribs down, and roast for 20 minutes.

4. Lower temperature to 325 degrees and roast an additional 18 minutes per pound for medium-rare meat (or 22 minutes per pound for medium). Insert a meat thermometer, and when the internal temperature reaches 115–120 degrees, remove roast from oven. Cover pan with foil so roast will continue cooking and let the juices seal. The meat is finished when its internal temperature has reached 125 degrees.

Horseradish Sauce

INGREDIENTS

1 cup sour cream

3 tablespoons prepared horseradish

2 teaspoons Dijon mustard

Combine all ingredients in a bowl and mix together. Add more horseradish if desired.

Beet & Apple Salad

INGREDIENTS

2 tablespoons honey

2 tablespoons apple cider vinegar

2 tablespoons olive oil

2 cans sliced beets

1 Fuji apple

1/4 cup crumbled blue cheese

1–2 teaspoons chopped parsley

1.   Make dressing: Whisk together honey, vinegar, and olive oil. Season with salt and pepper to taste. Set aside.

2.   Rinse and drain beets.

3.   Cut apple into slices.

4.   Toss beet and apple slices with dressing, coating well. Top with blue cheese and parsley.

Green Bean Bundles

INGREDIENTS

1 1/2 pounds fresh green beans

kitchen string

8–10 sprigs thyme

2 tablespoons butter

salt and pepper

1/2 cup pine nuts, lightly toasted

1.   Steam green beans for 3–4 minutes, until cooked but still firm. Plunge beans into ice water to keep their green color and stop them from cooking.

2.   Using kitchen string, make bundles of about 6–8 beans and a sprig of thyme.

3.   Heat butter in a sauté pan until nutty brown. Add green bean bundles and reheat for about a minute. Season with salt and pepper. Top with toasted pine nuts.

Mashed Root Vegetables

INGREDIENTS

2 parsnips

2 carrots

1 celery root

1 turnip

1 potato

salt

$1/2$ cup heavy cream

$1/2$ stick butter

4 sprigs thyme

3 garlic cloves, peeled

1.   Cut vegetables into large pieces and boil in salted water for 20 minutes or until very soft.

2.   While vegetables are cooking, heat cream and butter with thyme and garlic in a small saucepan until butter has melted. Remove from heat, cover, and let steep for 20 minutes.

3.   With a potato masher, mash all ingredients, adding steeped cream to desired consistency.

Shaved Fennel, Arugula, & Tangerine Salad

INGREDIENTS

1 recipe dressing (see below)

2 bulbs fennel, thinly sliced

1 can (15 ounces) tangerine or mandarin orange slices, drained

1 5-ounce bag baby arugula

Parmesan cheese

Dressing

2 teaspoons whole grain mustard

2 tablespoons white wine vinegar

6 tablespoons olive oil

2 garlic cloves, minced

salt and pepper

1.   Make dressing: Mix mustard and vinegar. Slowly whisk in oil to combine. Add minced garlic. Season with salt and pepper to taste.

2.   Toss fennel, tangerine slices, and arugula together with dressing when ready to serve.

3.   Shave Parmesan with vegetable peeler to top salad.

Delectable Pumpkin Cheesecake
with Chocolate Crust

INGREDIENTS

9 ounces chocolate wafers, finely crushed

¼ cup sugar

6 tablespoons butter, melted

1 ½ cups canned pumpkin, solid pack

½ cup light brown sugar

3 eggs, slightly beaten

5 ounces evaporated milk

1 teaspoon vanilla

½ cup sugar

1 tablespoon cornstarch

1 ½ teaspoons ground cinnamon

½ teaspoon ground ginger

¼ teaspoon ground nutmeg

¼ teaspoon ground cloves

salt

3–8 ounces mascarpone or cream cheese, softened

1. Preheat oven to 350 degrees. Mix chocolate wafer crumbs, sugar, and melted butter. Press mixture firmly onto the bottom of a 9-inch springform pan. Bake until crust is set, about 8–10 minutes. Remove from oven and cool crust completely.

2. In a bowl, stir together pumpkin, brown sugar, eggs, evaporated milk, and vanilla. Set aside.

3. In another large bowl, mix sugar, cornstarch, spices, and salt. Add cheese and beat on high speed until smooth. Take out ¼ of the cheese mixture and set aside for topping.

4. With mixer running at low speed, add pumpkin mixture to the cheese mixture and mix until combined and smooth.

5. Place springform pan with prepared crust on a baking sheet (in case it leaks). Pour pumpkin mixture into pan. Drop dollops of the reserved cheese mixture over the pumpkin mixture. Use a thin metal spatula or a knife to gently pull the cheese dollops through the pumpkin to make swirls.

6. Bake at 350 degrees for 50–60 minutes, or until center of cheesecake is just set. Remove from oven and cool for 30 minutes. Cover and chill for a couple of hours. Remove sides of springform pan to serve.

Autumn **Punch**

INGREDIENTS

2 whole cloves

$\frac{1}{2}$ whole vanilla bean, split in half

cheesecloth

string

64 ounces apple-cranberry juice

4 medium plums, pitted and sliced

1 bottle fruity white wine or
24 ounces ginger ale

1. Put cloves and vanilla in cheesecloth and tie
In a bundle with string.

2. Pour apple-cranberry juice into a large
container/pitcher. Add the plums and spice bag.

3. Cover and chill for 4–24 hours.

4. Remove spice bag. Stir in wine or ginger ale.
Either serve over ice with plum slices or heat
the punch and serve.

MAKE IT CHIC Spike apples with whole cloves
and float them in the punch.

Steamed green beans with toasted pine nuts

Fennel, arugula & tangerine salad

Food in Flight

Adorn your holiday buffet with hints of nature — label your holiday fare with elegant, graceful place cards that will answer all questions!

TOOLS
scissors
pen

MATERIALS
pinecones
spray glitter
artificial white doves from craft store
white paper
double-sided tape

1. Take your pinecones outside and coat them with a thin layer of spray glitter.

2. Back inside, place a pinecone on the table and perch a dove on top. Wrap the bird's wire legs around the pinecone to keep it steady. Repeat for the remaining doves and pinecones.

3. Cut slips of paper and write the names of your holiday dishes on them. Attach each slip to the wing of a dove with double-sided tape.

LITTLE DRUMMER BOY

Every year my mom would collect various holiday projects from her magazines and set up a giant table full of materials in the basement, and we would go to town assembling holiday crafts. After the fun with glue, glitter, and scissors, we would then pack the handmade goodies in boxes and mail them to our relatives as holiday treats. I do believe this is the point where it all began . . . I so enjoyed my role as a holiday elf that I am now blessed with a career inventing these projects. Start them early, start them young, 'cause nothing keeps kids more occupied than a big table chock-full of crafts-making materials — except maybe a table chock-full of crafty snacks! The next two recipes will tickle children's fancy because they can build the snack themselves, and one choice is sweet and the other choice is savory.

Create Your Own
Polenta Bar

MAKES 28 BARS

INGREDIENTS

parchment paper

3 cups chicken broth

1 cup milk

1/4 teaspoon salt

2 cups yellow cornmeal

1 tablespoon butter

1/3 cup Parmesan cheese

1 tablespoon melted butter

1. Line a 13x9x2-inch baking pan with parchment paper.

2. In a large saucepan, bring broth and milk to a boil. Add salt. Whisking constantly, add cornmeal in a slow, steady stream.

3. Cook over low heat, whisking occasionally, until polenta is thickened and bubbly. Remove pan from heat.

4. Add 1 tablespoon butter and Parmesan and whisk to mix well.

5. Pour polenta onto the parchment paper in the pan and spread evenly. Chill until firm, about 30 minutes to 1 hour.

6. To serve, brush with melted butter and broil for 3 minutes. Sprinkle with your choice of toppings (see below) and cut into bars.

IDEAS FOR TOPPINGS

sautéed mushrooms, onions, and parsley

Italian sausage and tomato sauce

shredded cheese and ham

cheddar cheese, sour cream, and bacon

Create Your Own
Cookie Bar

MAKES 20 BARS

INGREDIENTS

1 cup flour

$^1/_2$ cup rolled oats

$^1/_2$ teaspoon salt

3 sticks butter, softened

3 cups brown sugar

6 eggs

parchment paper

1. Preheat oven to 350 degrees.

2. Combine flour, rolled oats, and salt in a bowl. Set aside.

3. Using a mixer set on low speed, cream butter and sugar together. Add eggs, one at a time, combining well after each addition.

4. Carefully add flour mixture and continue mixing until dough forms.

5. Spread the cookie dough on a baking pan lined with parchment paper.

6. Sprinkle with your choice of toppings (see below). Bake in oven for 20-25 minutes. Cool and cut into bars.

IDEAS FOR TOPPINGS

chips (chocolate, peanut butter, butterscotch, and/or white chocolate)

nuts (walnuts, almonds, pecans, macadamias)

dried fruits (dates, cranberries, cherries, apricots)

flaked coconut

Sweet Imaginations

It's the holiday season, and while you are crazed with errands and preparations, your kids are out of school and wandering the house, looking for something to do. See where their imaginations take them when presented with a table full of fruits, candies, and cookies. Can 2 lemons equal a duck? Can a cookie become a cap? Can a piece of licorice become a scarf? See what little characters and creatures are born from their wild imaginations!

MATERIALS

glue

limes

lemons

oranges

kiwis

toothpicks

twigs

red licorice sticks

peppermints

marshmallows

cookies

chocolate chips

candy canes

candy buttons

any other foods that strike your fancy

SOME IDEAS ARE . . .

Duck

Stack two lemons on top of each other. Make a hat by cutting a marshmallow in half, and attach it to the "head" with a toothpick. Glue chocolate chips onto the duck's face for eyes and wrap a piece of licorice around its neck as a scarf.

Snowman

For the body, stack 3 oranges one on top of the other and fasten them together with toothpicks. Use multicolored candy canes for arms, a cookie for a hat, and candy sugar dots for buttons.

Deer

To make a deer with antlers, stick 2 thin twigs on the top of a kiwi. Glue a marshmallow to the back of the kiwi for a tail.

Note: These creatures contain food items, but don't eat them — they're just for show.

Mother Nature's
Holiday Home

Rather than indulge in all that candy when decorating your gingerbread house, try looking elsewhere for inspiration. Encourage your kids to get out of the house and gather treasures from Mother Nature — sticks, leaves, and pinecones can make wonderful holiday construction materials!

TOOLS
scissors
hot-glue gun

MATERIALS
boxes
craft glue
graham crackers
leaves
feathers
cedar bark
pinecones
berries
moss
glitter, sticks, twigs, etc.

There are so many ways to put together your home . . . here are some suggestions that should get you thinking.

1. Build your house's frame by stacking 3 empty boxes on top of one another.

2. Cover the exterior surface by gluing on graham crackers.

3. Build the roof by flattening an empty box, then folding it in half, creating a peak. Attach the 2 ends to the side of your building.

4. Cover the roof by gluing leaves, feathers, or cedar over the entire surface.

5. Glue a small pinecone on top for the chimney.

6. Glue small berries in the shape of a door. For the door's wreath, glue a pinch of moss to the center and embellish with a feather.

7. Frame out the windows using glitter sticks and glue white feathers inside the windows.

8. Glue thin twigs to frame the seams of the house, and layer moss at the base as shrubbery.

9. Stand a few large pinecones beside your house to act as a little forest.

Note: The house contains food items, but don't eat it — it's just for show. Some berries are poisonous.

INDEX

ACKNOWLEDGMENTS

It is humbling to once again think of the hard work and sacrifices made by the people who joined to make this book possible. From the bottom of my heart I thank all who contributed.

Amanda Kingloff, for the joy of watching you become one with your glue-gun.

Dalene Tarr, for never losing your determination to make it good.

Kerstin Sund, for going through so much personally and professionally to see this through.

Ali Dao McGann, girl, you simply rock.

Brice Gaillard, our shoot would have not been the same without you and your crowns.

Alfie Magby, for being the answer to my prayers.

Gary Tooth, "The Tooth," for really having an eye.

Paul Paul Paul Whicheloe . . . how do I count the ways?

Evan "Esther" McGann, for not saying much.

Emily Scofield and Stuart Gelwarg, for putting up with my moods and always being the calm in my storm.

Jill Cohen, Karen Murgolo, Kristen Schilo, and Bulfinch, for making me a priority.

Ira Silverberg, for never making me feel like I have to fight my own battles.

Stephanie Banyas, for trying to write the impossible recipes.

Bobby Flay, for continually telling me what time it is.

Luis Rivera, for once again being The Man.

Lynch's Garden Center, for the flowers that bloomed in December.

Brian Maynard, KitchenAid, All-Clad, and Lenox for continuing to provide me with the tools of my trade.

Francini, Franklin, Maria Fernanda, and Joshua Brenes; Charlie, Ralph, and Katherine Esposito; Pam and Nicholas Healey; CoCo Myers and Daniel, Harrison, Jensen, and Max Rowen . . . who showed up on a moment's notice and added life to our shots.

My mother, father, sisters, brother, aunts, uncles, and in-laws, for providing me with so many memories.

My husband, William, for his patience, evenness, humor, resilience . . . the list goes on and on. I love you.

And to my daughter, Prentiss, for making me realize the importance of having two treasured days.

Top row, left to right: Dalene Tarr, Luis Rivera, Brice Gaillard, and Amanda Kingloff. Bottom row, left to right: Ali Dao McGann, Kerstin Sund, and Alfie Magby.

Bedazzled & Bewildered

Candlelight is beautiful no matter what the setting, but surrounding a flame with glitter and sparkle this year will set the perfect, unique mood on your elegant holiday buffet!

TOOLS
scissors

MATERIALS
glue
large glass goblet vase
glitter-size glass marbles
silver ribbon
sparkly costume jewelry
votive candle

1. Working in sections, spread glue on the outside surface of the vase and attach the glittery marbles.
2. Glue the ribbon around the outside rim of the vase. Wrap more ribbon around the stem, covering it completely and ending it at the base with a knot.
3. Glue the jewelry to the rim.
4. Place the candle in the center of the vase.

A Candle Cocktail

What would the holidays be without the warm, flickering glow of candlelight?

MATERIALS
drinking glasses
silver garland of beads
taper candles

Fill each glass with silver beads and insert a candle taper.